MW01002047

7/0c

940.54   Donovan, William N.
DON   P.O.W. in the Pacific

11/98

\

p.o.w. in the pacific

p.o.w. in the pacific

*Memoirs of an
American Doctor in
World War II*

William N. Donovan, M.D.

Edited by
Josephine Donovan

with
Ann Devigne Donovan

A Scholarly Resources Inc. Imprint
Wilmington, Delaware

Scholarly Resources Inc.
104 Greenhill Avenue
Wilmington, DE 19805-1897

Sources for Illustrations
All illustrations owned by William Nelson Donovan except for
those in Chapters 3, 4, and 5: National Archives, College Park,
Maryland

Library of Congress Cataloging-in-Publication Data
Donovan, William N., 1910–
    P.O.W. in the Pacific : memoirs of an American doctor in
World War II / William N. Donovan ; edited by Josephine
Donovan with Ann Devigne Donovan.
        p.   cm.
    Includes bibliographical references.
    ISBN 0-8420-2725-4 (alk. paper)
    1. Donovan, William N., 1910–   . 2. World War, 1939–
1945—Prisoners and prisons, Japanese. 3. World War, 1939–
1945—Personal narratives, American. 4. Prisoners of War
—Taiwan—Biography. 5. Prisoners of war—United States—
Biography. 6. World War, 1939–1945—Medical care—United
States. 7. World War, 1939–1945—Medical care—Philippines.
8. United States. Army—Surgeons—Biography. I. Donovan,
Josephine, 1941–   . II. Donovan, Ann Devigne, 1951–   .
III. Title.
D805.T35D66   1998
940.54'7252'092—dc21   9748354
[B]   CIP

Editor's Note

*This book is dedicated
to my mother, Dode, whose graceful courage,
cheer, and dignity during the war and
in her own final battle with cancer
will always remain for us—alongside my
father's remarkable story—a source
of inspiration and pride.*

Acknowledgments

We would like to acknowledge the contributions and support that the following individuals made to this project: David C. Smith, Marilyn Emerick, Charlie Heaberlin, Richard Hancuff, Ann Romines, Niel Leksander, Katherine Leksander, Bill Donovan, the reference staffs at the University of Maine, Portsmouth Public Library, the National Archives, the Center of Military History, and Matthew R. Hershey and Michelle M. Slavin at Scholarly Resources.

Contents

Introduction

WORLD WAR II HAS BEEN called the greatest single event
in human history. Many studies and many memoirs—
especially of the war in Europe—have appeared. Less well
known is the story of the U.S. forces in the Pacific, and
comparatively little attention has been paid to the experience of American prisoners of war held by the Japanese. Many of their stories, which include some of the
most heinous atrocities of the war, have not been heard,
although a few (mostly privately printed) memoirs and
oral histories have appeared.

The memoirs presented here are those of my father,
William N. Donovan, who was then a captain in the U.S.
Army Medical Corps. He experienced firsthand many of
the decisive events in the war in the Philippines. Stationed
at Fort McKinley near Manila when the war broke out,
he worked as a battlefront doctor during the siege of
Bataan and Corregidor in the early months of 1942. He
was taken prisoner by the Japanese at the surrender of
Corregidor on May 6, 1942, and remained a POW until
late August 1945, shortly after V-J Day (August 14 in
the States).

During his captivity, my father was first interned in
the notorious Bilibid Prison in Manila. After several
months there, on February 27, 1943, he moved to
Camp #8, a smaller internment center in the port area
of Manila. On October 1, 1944, as the Allied forces under General Douglas MacArthur began their campaign
to recapture the Philippines, my father, along with

approximately eleven hundred other POWs, was shipped north to Formosa, via Hong Kong, in the hold of the Japanese freighter *Harō Maru*. The unspeakable conditions on this and the other so-called "hell ships" have justly been compared to those of the Middle Passage on African slave ships in the seventeenth and eighteenth centuries.

After his arrival in Formosa on November 9, 1944, my father was held in a camp in central Formosa (Taiwan) for the duration of the war. On September 6, 1945, after the camp's liberation, he was flown back to Manila, where he was finally able to cable my mother; it was the first time she had heard from him directly in about a year and a half. He returned to the United States by ship, landing in San Francisco on October 3, 1945; he was reunited with my mother and me (I was then four and a half years old) in Chicago on October 9. My mother and I had left the Philippines by ship in May of 1941, when I was two months old. The story of my mother's wartime experiences is included in Chapter 8.

My father was born on April 24, 1910, in Madison, Wisconsin, in the city's so-called "Bloody Fourth" (Irish) ward. His parents were Joseph Patrick Donovan, a doctor and Madison City Health Officer for many years, and Edith Nelson Donovan, a teacher of Greek and Latin in the Madison public schools. Of Norwegian parentage, my grandmother was one of the first female graduates of the University of Wisconsin, where she received a B.A. in the classics in 1899. The Donovan family had left Ireland during the Great Famine. My father's grandfather, Anthony, had arrived in Madison in 1858, served in the Union Army during the Civil War, and later became a municipal judge. He wrote a short memoir, *The Man and the Books: The Books and the Man* (1908), which, my father says, partly inspired him to record his own story.

My father attended St. Raphael's parochial school and Central High School in Madison, where he was a star basketball player; his team was a runner-up for the state championship in 1927. A February 2, 1927, newspaper account in the *Capitol Times* refers to Bill Donovan as a "scrappy forward"; during high school and college he worked as a lifeguard. He received his bachelor's degree from the University of Wisconsin in 1932 and his M.D. in 1936. He interned at Kings County Hospital in Brooklyn, New York, and at the U.S. Marine Hospital at Stapleton, Staten Island, New York. After a couple of years in the U.S. Public Health Service, he was commissioned as a regular army officer, a lieutenant, on July 14, 1939.

Bill and Dode Donovan, October 29, 1939, Fort Moultrie, South Carolina.

My mother, Josephine Devigne Donovan, was born on November 13, 1916, in New Rochelle, New York, of Irish and French parentage. She was raised in France and educated at Bryn Mawr College in Pennsylvania, where she received her bachelor's degree in history and graduated cum laude in 1938. She and my father were married in New York City on January 14, 1939. They moved to the Philippines, one of my father's first assignments, in the fall of 1940.

On December 7, 1941, the empire of Japan initiated hostilities in the Pacific with its air attack on the U.S. Pacific fleet anchored at Pearl Harbor, Oahu Island, Hawaii. In the aftermath, seven battleships were sunk, and one was left sinking. In addition, cruisers, destroyers, and other vessels were sunk or damaged, severely crippling U.S. naval forces in the Pacific. Three aircraft carriers, however, were out of port and thus escaped damage. They were instrumental in the tide-turning Battle of Midway on June 4–6, 1942, in which U.S. forces destroyed four Japanese carriers, more or less evening up the strength of the respective fleets. Meanwhile, the Japanese had attacked the Philippines, bombing air bases in the Manila area several hours after the attack on Pearl Harbor. For my father, the war began on December 8.

The United States had held the Philippines as a protectorate since the Spanish-American War in 1898. Prior to that, the Philippines had been a Spanish colonial possession since the sixteenth century. Under the 1934 Tydings-McDuffie Act, the Philippines were established as a commonwealth, a transitional status proposed for a decade, after which the islands were to become an independent nation. Until then the defense of the country was to remain under U.S. direction, which was the situation at the outbreak of the war, when Philippine units were under U.S. command.

On December 8, the day that the United States declared war on Japan, Japanese air strikes began on Guam and Wake Island, strategic U.S. installations between Hawaii and the Philippines. By the end of the month both were in Japanese hands. The Japanese invasion of the Philippines began on December 10, with a larger invasion, that at Lingayen Gulf on the island of Luzon, taking place on December 22.

The war in the Philippines, which settled onto the peninsula of Bataan and the island of Corregidor, is detailed in the introductions to Chapters 2 and 3. Suffice it to note here, however, that the heroic stand of U.S. and Filipino forces on Bataan and Corregidor in the spring of 1942 soon acquired legendary status. As historian Ronald H. Spector commented in 1985, "The defense of the Philippines . . . gave an enormous lift to American morale and will to win. The 'battling bastards of Bataan,' 'the Rock,' MacArthur's dramatic escape, the heroic doctors and nurses of Corregidor—all became part of American folklore."[1]

Meanwhile, the Japanese extended their conquests through Southeast Asia (Burma, Thailand, and French Indochina), capturing Singapore from the British on February 15, 1942, and moving through the South Pacific. By early in the summer of 1942, their holdings included Sumatra, Java, Borneo, and much of New Guinea. Historian Robert Leckie notes that after Pearl Harbor, "only in the Philippines, where the American-Filipino forces under Douglas MacArthur offered fierce resistance, was the Japanese timetable delayed."[2]

A possible invasion of Australia by the Japanese was frustrated by the naval Battle of the Coral Sea on May 7. After that battle, and the decisive Battle of Midway in early June, significant U.S. victories occurred on various islands scattered about the Pacific, including the Solomon Islands (November 12, 1942); Guadalcanal (February 9, 1943); Guam (August 10, 1944); Iwo Jima (March 16, 1945); and Okinawa (June 21, 1945).

On July 26, 1945, sixteen days after a successful test of the atomic bomb in New Mexico, and with an Allied invasion of Japan imminent, President Harry S. Truman announced the Potsdam Declaration, in which the Allies demanded the unconditional surrender of the Japanese, warning that otherwise "the utter destruction of the Japanese homeland" would ensue.[3] Since that surrender did not occur, the United States dropped an atomic bomb on Hiroshima on August 6 and a second on Nagasaki three days later. On August 15, the emperor of Japan announced his country's unconditional surrender. Formal surrender ceremonies took place on September 2, with General MacArthur presiding, on the U.S. battleship *Missouri* in Tokyo Bay.

Before the war started, President Franklin D. Roosevelt, at the suggestion of the U.S. Chief of Naval Operations, Admiral Harold Stark, and with the encouragement of British prime minister Winston Churchill, had reluctantly adopted a "Europe first" policy. The primary war effort was to be in the European theater, leaving the U.S. forces in the Pacific to conduct a holding operation until industrial production and manpower recruitment allowed a full-fledged buildup there. The net effect of this policy was to abandon Allied forces in the Pacific, then under Japanese siege, to their own resources. For the American troops in the Philippines this meant that, despite perhaps wishful reassurances from MacArthur, no reenforcements or supplies would be forthcoming. Indeed, on December 8 four troopships bound for Manila were ordered back to San Francisco, and another convoy with men and supplies was diverted to the Fiji Islands.

After the war, five thousand Japanese military and civilian officials were brought to trial for war crimes. Nine hundred were executed, most for atrocities committed against Allied POWs. My father provided a deposition for these trials, which were held between 1945 and 1951. Extended excerpts from this deposition, which is now in the National Archives, are included in the Appendix. After the war, a few Americans were tried for treason. My father also testified at one such trial, that of Sgt. David Provoo in New York City in the fall of 1952.

This project would never have come to fruition without the labors of my sister, Ann Donovan, who prompted my father with questions and then recorded and transcribed his answers, which I then edited. The recording was done over several sessions during the late fall and early winter of 1995–96. While we had long planned to record my father's war memoirs—stories that my sister, my brother Bill, my mother, and I had heard many times—the final impetus came during the events commemorating the fiftieth anniversary of V-J Day in August 1995. As I listened to historians' reflections, I realized that my father's account could add much to the historical record. For example, the horrible episode aboard the prison ship *Harō Maru* in which several prisoners were killed by other POWs is recounted somewhat differently by my father (see Chapter 5) than by Gavan Daws in his *Prisoners of the Japanese.*[4]

My editing of these memoirs consisted in organizing the material chronologically, deleting repetitions, providing smooth transitions, and adding historical background. Very little of my father's wording has been changed, however; the text stands much as he spoke it or added to it in later conversations. In the interest of historical authenticity, the term "Jap" has been retained. Although no longer acceptable, it was commonly used during the war and helps to convey the mood of the times.

Wherever possible, I have corroborated my father's account with existing historical records and other memoirs. In this way I was able to clear up minor factual inconsistencies. However, as noted, my father's recollections of events occasionally diverge from the version of others who experienced the same events; historians will have to choose among the facts. One final editorial note: As editor I refer to my father in the third person as Captain Donovan in the chapter introductions, but in the introduction to Chapter 7 and in Chapter 8, which concerns our family during the war, I revert to the first person.

The horror and shock of the atomic devastation of Hiroshima and Nagasaki have eclipsed in the historical memory the horror and magnitude of Japanese atrocities during World War II, which have been called the "forgotten holocaust."[5] But neither those crimes nor Hiroshima should be forgotten. For to forget the evils of the past is to invite their repetition. It is my hope that this memoir will contribute to our understanding and memory of this dark period in human history. My father has always maintained that it was largely a matter of luck that he survived. But I think these memoirs demonstrate that discipline, courage, intelligence, determination, and, last but not least, a powerful sense of humor also played their part.

J. D.

Notes

1. Ronald H. Spector, *Eagle against the Sun: The American War with Japan* (New York: Free Press, 1985), 139. Other works consulted in the preparation of this book, but not mentioned elsewhere, include John S. Coleman, Jr., *Bataan and Beyond: Memories of an American POW* (College Park: Texas A&M Press, 1978); Betty B. Jones, *The December Ship* (Jefferson, NC: McFarland, 1992); Robert S. LaForte et al., eds., *With Only the Will to Live: Accounts of Americans in Japanese Prison Camps, 1941–1945* (Wilmington, DE: Scholarly Resources, 1984); Judy Barrett Litoff and David C. Smith, eds., *Since You Went Away: World War II Letters from American Women on the Home Front* (New York: Oxford University Press, 1991);

Lawrence Taylor, *A Trial of Generals: Homma, Yamashita, MacArthur* (South Bend, IN: Icarus Press, 1981); and William M. Tuttle, Jr., *"Daddy's Gone to War": The Second World War in the Lives of America's Children* (New York: Oxford University Press, 1993).

2. Robert Leckie, *Delivered from Evil: The Saga of World War II* (New York: Harper and Row, 1987), 345.

3. Ibid., 578.

4. For Forrest Knox's account, see Gavan Daws, *Prisoners of the Japanese: POWs of World War II in the Pacific* (New York: William Morrow, 1994), 289–91, 297–99.

5. Arnold Brackman, *The Other Nuremberg: The Untold Story of the Tokyo War Crimes Trials* (New York: William Morrow, 1987), 17.

1

The War Begins

AT 3:30 A.M. ON DECEMBER 8, 1941, radio broadcasts in the Philippines were interrupted with the news of the attack on Pearl Harbor. By noon, Japanese bombs were falling on U.S. air bases in the Philippines, destroying much of the American air fleet, which then consisted of more than thirty B-17s and one hundred P-40 fighter planes. Historians now agree that the Philippines were probably lost in those first few hours, because without an air fleet, the islands were indefensible. On December 10 the U.S. naval base at Cavite near Manila was also virtually destroyed.

The Japanese landed troops on Luzon on December 10 and 12, and on Mindanao, in the southern Philippines, on December 20. The main invasion force, however, under Lt. Gen. Mashaharu Homma, landed at Lingayen Gulf on Luzon on December 22. General MacArthur's troops at the time consisted of approximately 31,000 well-trained regular forces composed of both Americans and Filipinos (12,000 of the men were the crack Philippine Scouts) in addition to a largely reserve, poorly trained, and poorly equipped Philippine army of approximately 100,000. In December 1941 these forces were divided into two sectors: the North Luzon Force under Maj. Gen. Jonathan M. Wainwright, and the South Luzon Force under Maj. Gen. George M. Parker, Jr. There was also a contingent composed largely of artillery forces based on Corregidor, under the command of Maj. Gen. George Moore. The Japanese invasion force numbered approximately 43,000.

MacArthur had intended to repulse the invading forces at the landing beaches, but when that plan proved unsuccessful he reverted to an earlier strategy, the so-called War Plan Orange. MacArthur's WPO-3 involved moving all of his troops to the peninsula of Bataan on southern Luzon, where he hoped to engage in a six-month

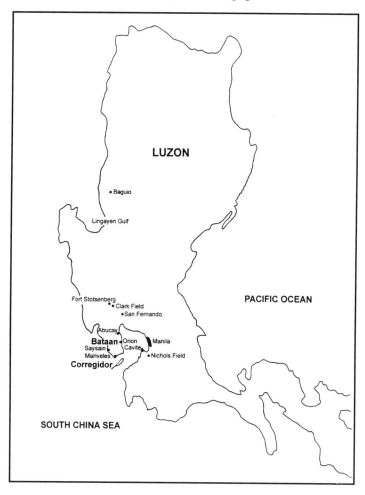

holding action until re-enforcements could arrive for a counterattack against the Japanese. The Japanese plan had been to take the Philippines in fifty days. While the Allied forces were ultimately defeated, "the valiant American defense of Bataan held up Japan for several months," one historian notes, a delay that "may well have . . . saved Australia."[1]

After the Lingayen Gulf landing, the Japanese forces advanced rapidly toward Manila. They were delayed long enough, however, by Wainwright's men for most of the American forces to move to Bataan—but not long enough for sufficient supplies (to feed approximately 120,000 men and civilian refugees for six months) also to be relocated. The supplies on hand were only sufficent to feed such numbers for one month.

The evacuation to Bataan, which one observer said "looked like a small Dunkirk,"[2] has been described by historians as a minor miracle, strategically important in delaying the Japanese advance through the western Pacific by several months. John Toland remarks that "the chances of a successful withdrawal to the peninsula seemed hopeless to many. . . . Manila Bay was dotted with slow-moving barges, pleasure steamers, launches, and tugs shuttling men, munitions, and food to Corregidor and Bataan. Highway 3 north out of Manila was jammed with trucks . . . buses, cars, cartelas, and oxcarts."[3] As Robert Leckie observes, "MacArthur's forces executed the . . . movement with masterly skill. . . . By this decision and movement, MacArthur averted immediate defeat [and] delayed the Japanese timetable by four months."[4]

On Christmas Eve the American headquarters in Manila was evacuated. General MacArthur and his family, as well as the president of the Philippines, Manuel Quezon, and the U.S. high commissioner to the Philippines, Francis B. Sayre, and their staffs retreated to

Corregidor. On December 26, MacArthur declared Manila an "open city," which under international law meant that it was to be spared military destruction, a status ignored by General Homma, who, after the war, was tried, convicted, and executed. By January 2, Japanese forces had taken the city.

Calumpit Bridge over the unfordable Pampanga River, a strategic link to Bataan about thirty miles north of Manila, was blown up on orders of General Wainwright at 6:15 A.M. on New Year's Day, just as Japanese troops reached it. On January 5 another strategic bridge—at Layac, to the north—was also destroyed. WPO-3 had worked. The bulk of the U.S. forces had made it to Bataan, and the three-month siege of the peninsula began.

Captain Donovan was stationed at Fort McKinley near Manila when the war began but was reassigned to Sternberg General Hospital from December 12 to 26, after which he joined the 2d Battalion, 45th Infantry Regiment (PS), in Bataan. He crossed over the Calumpit Bridge on a return trip to Bataan from Manila just hours before it was destroyed.

"In the spring of 1941 we were put on alert; we were pretty close to war with Japan. The Navy had evacuated all their dependents about eighteen months before, and finally the Army decided that the families had to go home. They could go to two places: San Francisco or New York City (you would go home through the Panama Canal). I signed my wife, Dode, up for San Francisco because I knew it was going to be an awful trip for her with Josie just two months old; she was born in March and they went back in May.

Life was very pleasant in the Philippines until the wives were evacuated. Dode and Josie left Manila on

May 14 on the USAT *Washington*. It was a very sad day, really. I went up on shipboard to say good-bye. I carried Josie around the deck for a while and then finally we had to get off. I drove down Dewey Boulevard, which bordered the bay, and I got out of the car and went over and stood under a tree and watched the ship sail away, out past Corregidor Island, until it was out of sight. I tell you that was about the saddest day I ever put in. I knew it was going to be a long haul, but I didn't realize how bad it would get. When I got back to the post, there were just no sounds at all. It was just dead. Previously there had been kids playing around and making noise, but there were no children there, no wives, no nothing.

After the dependents left, we officers had to double up. They didn't charge us for quarters. Everything was free. Ken Hagen and I lived together for a while. He was an ENT [eyes, nose, and throat] specialist. Then he was ordered down to Sternberg Hospital in Manila. So that left me alone for a short while. Two officers in another group were ordered to Corregidor and that left Captain Joe Peters alone, so he came and asked me if I'd like to move in with him. He had a much better setup than I had, although the location of his place was much hotter, on the other side of the post, Fort McKinley. Finally, we ended up there with three of us living together: Peters, Bill DeBakey, and myself.

We had two Filipino cooks and I tell you they were good cooks. For breakfast they'd give you these small rolls with cinnamon and sugar and, Jesus, they were good. Then we'd have a light lunch and then for dinner we'd have either a chicken or a turkey with all the trimmings to go with it, really a big, big meal. We also had a *lavendero* who did all of our laundry. You can wear your clothes only once out there. So you'd put a uniform on in the morning—a clean uniform—and then when you got home at noon you'd take it off and throw it in the corner and put on some sports clothes. Then the *lavendero*, she'd wash the uniform and press it. I had two or three uniforms. They were cotton, long-sleeved. We didn't wear a tie. MacArthur had started that. It used to be you'd have to wear a tie. Then in the afternoon we'd always take a siesta. In fact, you weren't allowed out of your quarters until three o'clock unless you had some official business. It was just an army rule that you weren't allowed out. At three o'clock people would suddenly appear on the golf course.

About a week before the war started we were put on intensified alert; we had to stay within twenty minutes of the post. It was about a twenty-minute drive to Manila, so we felt that we could go there for movies. It happened that one time we sat right behind MacArthur. MacArthur went to a movie every day, but he would always leave a little bit early. A friend of mine, Ken Hagen, said, "Let's watch for the security when MacArthur leaves." So we went out and saw he had three or four guards stationed around; a sedan came up at a very high speed and stopped. Just then MacArthur walked out and got in the car, and off he went.

Before the war started, there were a couple of guys living next to us by the name of Morgan and Murphy. On weekends they'd have these wild parties; they'd send down to Manila for these supposed models. About ten o'clock at night a couple of cabs full of women, all dressed in formal clothes, would arrive. These two—Morgan and Murphy—they'd make the goddamnedest racket. All night long, they'd walk around banging on a pan with a stick. So when the war started and I heard this racket about three A.M., I thought it was Murphy and Morgan over there making their usual noise.

I had a radio right next to my bed. I hadn't used it in months, but for some reason that morning I reached over and turned it on and the news came on that we were at war with Japan. Pearl Harbor had been bombed, and we had taken a tremendous loss there. They had sunk five ships and they had killed several thousand troops, and Roosevelt had announced that he was going to address the Congress, which he did that morning, "a day that will live in infamy." So the war was on. It was kind of a strange feeling because we knew we were at war but we didn't have any orders. We didn't know what the hell we were supposed to do. We felt we should be wearing our field uniforms, but we still had on our regular uniforms because we hadn't received any orders to the contrary. So the next day we just got up and went to work just as usual.

The morning after Pearl Harbor, December 8, about 9 A.M., the adjutant in the hospital at Fort McKinley said, "We've got word that we're going to have a bombing raid here. There are about thirty Jap bombers heading this way. They'll be here in less than half an hour. We want to get patients off the second floor of the hospital and get them at least to the ground floor." We moved the patients, and soon began to get casualties.

They bombed the airfields and destroyed most of our planes. MacArthur got blamed for that, but it wasn't his doing. He ordered all the planes up. I knew one of the gunners on one of those planes. He said once they were up they got orders to return. They were headed south and got orders to turn around and come back. These were false orders, of course, put out by the Japanese in English. So they landed and had lunch. Then the Jap planes came by and wiped out the fleet.

That night they strafed the post. The Japs were coming in off aircraft carriers. There were no lights on; the post was black. It was empty because they had moved the army out; they knew we were going to be bombed.

A day or two after the war started they bombed Cavite, a Navy base about seven to eight miles from Manila on the bay. The Navy had taken no precautions as far as getting things out of the way in case of a bombing, and so they took terrible casualties. I happened to be down at Sternberg Hospital in Manila when the trucks began arriving from Cavite. That was the goddamnedest mess you ever saw. Bodies were piled onto trucks with arms or legs missing, some were dead. All of them piled together. It looked like a meat factory. Jesus, what a bloody mess that was!

The plan had been in case of war to go to Bataan, a peninsula west of Manila. All American troops were supposed to go to Bataan. The Allied forces were divided into two groups there—a northern group and a southern group. The southern group had to come up and go through Manila and then get to Bataan. MacArthur had changed that plan, though; he was originally going to meet the Japs at the beach, and try not to give up an inch of territory without fighting for it. But the Japs sent in an overwhelming force, and he had to abandon his plan and go back to the old WPO-3, they called it, War Plan Orange. So the Japs attacked the Philippines. We knew they had a battle fleet out. To start we didn't know whether they were going to go south, but soon it was apparent that they were coming to the Philippines. So they landed on Luzon, and, as I say, MacArthur wanted to meet them at the beach, but we had to give that up. The rest of us went to Bataan, which was fairly easy to defend. Before the war started we had gone on ten-day maneuvers over there several times.

One time we went on reconnaissance near Lingayen beach where the Japs later landed and where MacArthur landed when he returned. It was just a natural place for a landing. The water was full of stingrays there. They can give you a hell of a sting. Luckily we saw them in time and weren't too eager to go in swimming.

Usually on these prewar maneuvers on Bataan I had nothing to do, so I used to go out and wander around. Sometimes I'd take the ambulance out and ride around the countryside. Once I found a stream there and a little waterfall. The water was just about up to my neck. As soon as I found that, I used to go up there and go swimming every day, and I'll tell you that gives you an appetite, and we had plenty of food, so by the time the war started I was in pretty good shape. I'd been swimming every day, sometimes twice a day, and we had all the food that we wanted to eat. But then along in January, after the fighting had begun on Bataan, they were running out of food and had to cut the rations. They had planned on just one division being on Bataan. Instead of that there were a hundred thousand people there, and a bunch of Filipinos, and we had to feed them. So they cut the food ration. We had two meals a day and none at noon. The place was full of mosquitoes and also full of malaria. We doctors were giving out quinine every day as a prophylactic. We used to sleep under a mosquito bar, largely to keep the monkeys out. There'd be hundreds of them. When you'd shave in the morning there'd be hundreds of monkeys looking at you. They never bothered us, but if they'd gotten mad at you they could have killed you easily. I'd go out in the morning to shave. I had a Filipino *hancho* who'd have hot water for me. About 6:00 in the morning, he'd just be standing there, so that I could shave.

About a month or so before the war started, while we were on maneuvers in Bataan, Colonel Ross Smith, my commanding officer, had put out an order: "There will be no liquor on this maneuver." I didn't get that message, so I brought—I always brought a good supply of liquor on maneuvers—a bottle of bourbon, a bottle of scotch, and a bottle of this Pennsylvania whiskey. We were stopped for dinner and General Edward King—he was the commanding general of Bataan, next under Wainwright—was having dinner with our regiment. They said he always wanted a drink before dinner. So this regimental colonel sent his aide over to me, and he asked if we had any "medicinal liquor," and I said, "Yeah, what kind would you want—bourbon, scotch, or rye?"

He said, "A bottle of Scotch will be fine."

So I handed him one: "You can have a bottle of Scotch."

Then they came back and he said, "The colonel invites you to have dinner with him."

"Fine."

So I went and had dinner with him and the general.

The next morning they were going to go up on some reconnaissance flights. They had three planes. So the regimental colonel put me on a plane, and there was a plane on either side of us. We started off and the one on the right started smoking and went down. It crashed. We got up, though, and flew all around the area and out over the Pacific. I was down in the hold of the plane—the bomb bay area—and we suddenly started going straight down. We just went straight down, straight down, and were turning around! I thought, well, this is it! When he got way down, though, he leveled it off and landed it. We landed there at Clark Field. We got off and went in to Fort Stotsenburg. I knew the C.O. [Commanding Officer] there. We talked for a minute and had lunch, and then we got back in the plane.

When we were flying around over Bataan, I could see that you couldn't see anything down below, that you couldn't make out any individuals at all, because they were all lost in the jungle. When we were in Bataan later in the jungle war, I knew that the Jap planes couldn't bother us, couldn't see us, but the rest of them didn't know that. When a plane would come over, they'd all hit the ground, but I never paid any attention to it. I just kept walking around. Once we were all eating there at a table, and some Jap planes came over and, Jeez, the rest of them they all hit the ground and started carrying on, and I sat there and finished. I knew damn well they couldn't see us. So I sat there and finished lunch and later on when we were going down this trail that ran to the ocean, we were targeted again, but again I knew that the Japs couldn't see us, and I just walked standing up. I got a reputation for being sort of fearless, but I knew damn well that we could stand up and do whatever we wanted and the Jap planes couldn't see us. The rest of them didn't seem to realize that.

There were two main fronts. First we had a front meeting the Japs, who were coming down through the lowlands of the Philippines. After they had landed up in Lingayen Gulf, which was on December 22, they marched south, and we tried to slow them down a bit, but finally we had to get over to Bataan. They had to hold the line so that this unit from the south could come through and go to Bataan, and they did that, which saved about half of the Army. In the meantime, our unit had moved over to Bataan just before Christmas, and shortly thereafter we heard that some of the units were sending back to Manila and bringing a lot of food and liquor and stuff out of there. So I said to the C.O., "I'd just as soon take a trip back to Manila, take a staff car, or I'll take my own car, but I'll have a staff car follow me, in case we get stuck." It was the 31st of December. I had my little car out there, an old '34 V-8 Ford that I had paid sixty-four bucks for in New York. I'd had it painted brown, so it looked like an army car; I got in, and I had this staff car following me. I told him to stick close to me, and we drove into Manila.

Manila was a hell of a jam—all kinds of vehicles of every description. When we got there we went out to Fort McKinley, and, of course, McKinley was empty. I didn't realize it at the time but the Japs were right around— they had the place circled—they entered the place the next morning. But Colonel Smith said, "Stay overnight if you want. You can eat a good dinner there at the Officers' Club." I went out to McKinley first of all and to my quarters to pick up some stuff. The Filipinos had been through it, though, looting. Everything was a shambles. I found a few things that I wanted. I found a couple of pipes and a few odds and ends and then I stopped at the post office. They were just closing up for good.

The clerk said, "I'm just closing up. You're here just in time. Here's a Christmas present from someone." It was a present from Dode, a briefcase, which I still have, though it's full of bullet holes. So I took that and then I drove around McKinley. I wanted to get some shoes, so I went out to where they stored all these shoes, and I found a pair that fit. All I had was a flashlight and I was there alone. I thought, "Jees, what a hell of a place to be all by yourself." I got the hell out of there, and got in the car and drove back downtown. I had dinner at the Officers' Club, but it was nearly empty. And then I stopped by Sternberg Hospital and ran into a good friend of mine, Captain Steve Sitter; he and a lieutenant colonel were sitting there right at the entrance. Steve said, "What the hell are you doing here?" I said I came back to get some booze and mail, go to the Officers' Club, and get a dinner. He said, "You better get out of here. We're going to have to be down at the dock at midnight. We're going to

Corregidor. Manila will be an empty city. It's undefended. The Japs will be here tomorrow morning, in fact maybe before then."

So I got three bottles of liquor. I could have taken— I should have taken—a lot more, because the next day the whole thing blew up. They were shipping all the liquor from the Officers' Club on a boat out to Corregidor, but it hit a mine and blew up. All that liquor was lost. Another boat was lost too, a bunch of politicians trying to get away. They were trying to get to Corregidor, and they didn't know anything about all those mines, so they got blown up too. Manila Bay was full of sharks, too. You could see them swimming around. They used to throw the garbage out every night on Corregidor and those sharks would come around. I counted twenty-six of them one night. It wouldn't have been a healthy place to go swimming, I'll tell you that, if they were hungry.

I went back to the car and told the driver of the staff car to keep close behind me. There was a gas station still open, so we filled up both cars and started off. I had to go up through a town called San Fernando, and when I got there, there was a row of tanks lined up firing, and I stopped and talked to an officer. He said, "Do you want a cup of coffee? You can get a cup of coffee here if you want it." I had a cup of coffee.

"What's going on up here?" I asked.

"Oh, the Japs are out there," he said. "Why, where are you headed for?"

"Bataan," I said.

"You'd better get going, 'cause they're going to be cutting off that bridge. We're going to pull that bridge in another hour or so."

There were two bridges that I had to go across to get to Bataan.

"Once they blow," he said, "you can't get to Bataan. You'd better get going."

I got in my old Ford, and I drove just as fast as it would go, with the staff car following me, and we went up and around through San Fernando and then down the long drive to Bataan. It was about a twenty-five-mile drive. We were stopped by sentries a couple of times, our own sentries, and they would say "hurry on," "get going," and we finally got back to Bataan.

At one point there was a hell of a hill you had to go up. It's just an immense hill, and the car wouldn't go up in first; it wasn't powerful enough. The way I got over that hill was to speed the engine up as fast as it could go, then let the clutch in, and that would push me ahead about ten yards. Then I'd come to a stop and do it over again. I finally got over the hill. The other guy following me didn't have much trouble getting over the hill.

Colonel Smith had told me to wake him up when I got back from Manila. He was interested in the liquor. He said, "Wake me up. I don't care what time you get back," because we had stopped at the Officers' Club and gotten some whiskey for him. When I got back, I went to the headquarters and found Smith. He didn't say anything, not a word. I just handed him the whiskey that he had ordered, and he took off the top and drank about half a bottle right off the bat. After he finished, he said, "How was your trip? I thought maybe you were going to stay there."

So I got back to Bataan just in time. They blew up the bridge the next morning, New Year's Day. And the Japs took Manila and San Fernando on January 2. Later, when the fighting started on Bataan I had to abandon that old Ford. I hid it in the jungle. I drove it off the road and covered it over with branches. For all I know, it's still there."

Notes

1. William L. O'Neill, *A Democracy at War: America's Fight at Home and Abroad in World War II* (New York: Free Press, 1993), 117.

2. Donald Knox, *Death March: The Survivors of Bataan* (New York: Harcourt, 1981), 33.

3. John Toland, *But Not in Shame: The Six Months after Pearl Harbor* (New York: Random House, 1961), 124.

4. Leckie, *Delivered from Evil*, 352.

2

Bataan

THE SIEGE OF BATAAN BEGAN in early January 1942 and ended on April 9, 1942, when the U.S. forces under Maj. Gen. Edward P. King, Jr., surrendered. At the beginning of January the American troops numbered approximately 15,000; they were fighting alongside approximately 65,000 Filipinos. By the surrender the total force was between 76,000 and 78,000, of which 11,500 to 12,000 were Americans.

Bataan is a peninsula nearly five hundred square miles in area, dominated by two jungle-covered mountains— extinct volcanoes—Mount Natib and Mount Bataan. The low-lying areas were characterized by tall cane and thick clumps of bamboo. There were two main roads: one around the perimeter; the other, the Pilar-Bagac Highway, cut through the center between the mountains.

Despite the heroic efforts that had been made in the latter part of December to transport food, medicine, and supplies to Bataan from the Manila area, they proved inadequate. On January 5, rations to the troops were cut in half, and in March they were reduced to a third. This meant that in January rations averaged about two thousand calories per person a day; they were down to fifteen hundred calories in February and to about one thousand in March. Half-rations meant 3.7 ounces of rice, 1.8 ounces of sugar, 1.2 ounces of canned milk,

2.44 ounces of canned fish, and an occasional can of vegetables.[1] This was supplemented infrequently by slaughtered unit horses, carabao, lizards, and monkeys. Medical supplies also were badly lacking.

Two general hospitals were established in the southeast corner of the peninsula. Although they were marked with white crosses visible from the air, one of them, hospital #1 at Little Baguio, was bombed by the Japanese on two occasions: March 30 and April 7. A total of one hundred patients and personnel were killed and two hundred wounded. In addition, there were several smaller field hospitals. At the time of the surrender there were twenty-four thousand patients in all of these installations. In addition to battle wounds, a heavy toll was taken by malnutrition, malaria, and intestinal diseases such as dysentery. By early April "approximately 80 percent of the front line troops had malaria, 75 percent suffered from dysentery, and about 35 percent had beriberi."[2] Captain Donovan had all three at one time or another during the siege of Bataan.

What is called the First Battle of Bataan took place from January 9 to 23. Captain Donovan was attached to the 45th Infantry Regiment (Philippine Scouts), first as 2d Battalion Surgeon and later as Regimental Surgeon. The 45th was under the command of Col. Thomas W. Doyle, and the 2d Battalion was under Lt. Col. Ross B. Smith.

The 45th first engaged the enemy on January 18 in the area of the Abucay Hacienda as re-enforcements on the so-called first line of defense, the "Abucay line," which ran along the Balantay River from Abucay on the east to Maubun on the west. For several days these units "attacked aggressively and fiercely," according to one historian, but by January 21 they "were bogged down in dense vegetation."[3]

Louis Morton chronicles the 45th Division's activities during the First Battle of Bataan as follows: At 5 P.M. on January 16 the unit left its bivouac area but soon "lost its way."[4] It finally reached its destination on the defense line in the predawn hours of January 18, the objective being the Balantay River. The 2d Battalion (Captain Donovan's unit) reached the river early in the afternoon of January 19. Intense fighting in "dense vegetation" ensued the next two days, with the Japanese forces counterattacking on the 22d.[5] By nightfall on January 22, the troops of the 45th Division remained in "approximately the same place they had been five days earlier when they began the counterattack. They had been in action almost continuously during these five days and the strain of combat was clearly evident. The men on the front line had received little water or food and practically no hot meals during the battle."[6]

On January 22, MacArthur decided to retreat to the so-called second defense line (under WPO-3), which was just south of the Pilar-Bagac Highway. A general retreat began on January 23 with units of the 45th (including Captain Donovan's) ordered to provide a protective shell to enable the other units to withdraw. They were successful in providing the shell—an orderly retreat ensued—but at a price. When on January 24 the shell troops passed before a protective line of tanks, they looked like "walking dead men," according to eyewitnesses. "Unwashed and unshaven for nine days, their starved faces were expressionless."[7]

Captain Donovan received the Distinguished Service Cross—the highest decoration after the Congressional Medal of Honor—for events that occurred during this battle. The award is given for "extraordinary heroism" in combat. According to the citation order, which was personally approved by General MacArthur before he left the Philippines and signed by Maj. Gen. R. K. Sutherland, MacArthur's chief of staff, "When the unit to which he was assigned was subjected to an intense concentration of hostile rifle and mortar fire on January 20, Captain Donovan displayed conspicuous courage and devotion to duty by his sustained efforts under fire in the front lines in administering to casualties and arranging for the evacuation of the more seriously wounded. . . . His valiant efforts were productive in saving the lives of many." A similar incident occurred on February 11.

In a chronology of events that Captain Donovan made during the war, he noted that his unit went on January 27 "to Apalama, Anyasan, and Silaiim sector. Remained there to 15 Feb." This operation became known as the Battle of the Points. As U.S. forces regrouped along the Bagac-Orion line, the Japanese launched several "small amphibious assaults against 'the points,' narrow fingers of land jutting out from the southwest tip of the Bataan peninsula far behind the main defense line."[8]

After these landings, significant battles occurred during the three-week period from late January to mid-February near the Saysain and Tuol Rivers and at Quinauen Point, in which the U.S. forces successfully contained the Japanese offensive. A counterattack by the 2d Battalion (in conjunction with the 57th Infantry Regiment) on February 12 along the Mount Pucot line was considered especially successful.[9] Morton notes that in late January Captain Donovan's unit was instrumental in preventing a Japanese breakthrough to the West Road: "The situation was saved . . . when the Scouts of the 2d battalion, 45th Infantry, arrived on the scene, led by their executive officer, Capt. Arthur C. Biedenstein."[10] Unfortunately, however, on January 30, friendly fire killed several Scouts: "Either the battalion's front line had been incorrectly reported to the artillery or plotted inaccurately, for the result was almost disastrous. . . . The Scouts soon found themselves under fire from their own guns. Before the artillery command post could be reached, four Scouts had been killed and fourteen more wounded."[11]

By January 31, Morton observes, the 2d Battalion "was in poor shape. It had reached the Anyasan-Silaiim sector after a grueling march from Abucay, where it had been badly mauled. One of its companies had been hard hit and disorganized from friendly artillery, and casualties throughout the battle had been heavy."[12] In a February 2 attack under Lt. Col. Ross B. Smith, the 2d Battalion held the northern flank along the Silaiim River and successfully seized the mouth of the river and the northern sector of Silaiim Point. On February 12, under heavy machine-gun fire, and on February 13, the 2d Battalion achieved its mission of pushing the Japanese forces back to the beach.

The unit, which had been in continuous action since January 29, "had borne the brunt of the final counterattack" with twenty-six men killed and forty-two wounded.[13] General MacArthur's biographer, D. Clayton James, termed the Battle of the Points "the bloodiest fighting yet seen on Luzon . . . terminat[ing] in Japanese defeats."[14] The 45th Division became known during these actions, one scholar notes, for its "disinclination to take prisoners" because its men had discovered Scout corpses mutilated and found Japanese prisoners to be treacherous.[15]

During a lull in the fighting in February, the Japanese received massive re-enforcements, while the Americans received none. MacArthur said ruefully, "I could only bury my dead," as the Japanese redoubled their strength.[16] Meanwhile, Captain Donovan was hospitalized from February 27 to March 7 and from March 18 to 27 for malaria and dysentery. Although he had been discharged, he was still on the hospital grounds on March 30 when the hospital was bombed by the Japanese.

The Second Battle of Bataan occurred along the second defense line from March 15 to April 9, with the final siege beginning April 3 and culminating with the U.S. surrender on April 9. During these final days, the 45th Infantry was successful in penetrating Japanese lines (Morton notes, on April 6, Colonel Doyle's men "had made the only gains of the day").[17] On the next day the unit was ambushed: "At the first burst of fire Colonel Doyle had gone forward to take command. The situation was confused and the units disorganized, but Doyle kept his men in action until . . . daylight," after which a withdrawal commenced.[18] Captain Donovan received the Silver Star for "gallantry in action . . . on April 7, 1942." The citation order notes that during "intense enemy fire . . . this courageous officer maintained his . . . humanitarian task in the front lines . . . with the result that many . . . were saved . . . and with the further result that his example of devotion to duty . . . served as a vivid inspiration to the personnel of his unit."

Shortly thereafter, during the night of April 8–9, two thousand Americans escaped from Bataan to Corregidor on small boats, Captain Donovan among them. He thus narrowly missed the infamous Death March of approximately sixty thousand American and Filipino POWs that began on April 10. During the sixty-five-mile trek several thousand died under atrocious conditions, including nearly one thousand Americans (of the approximately nine thousand on the march). After the war the Death March was another of the war crimes for which Japanese generals were tried and executed.

In 1945, on the recapture of Bataan and Corregidor, General MacArthur called Bataan "one of the decisive battles of the war." The "long protracted struggle" there

gave the Allied forces in the Pacific time to provide for
the defense of Australia and to regroup and resupply,
which was crucial to the ultimate victory. Although defeated, he continued, "no army in history more thor-
oughly accomplished its mission. Let no man henceforth
speak of it other than as a magnificent victory."[19]

"The Philippine division consisted of three regiments:
There was the 45th Infantry commanded by Col.
Thomas Doyle; the 57th Infantry, which had been the
Philippine Scouts, that was commanded by four different commanders; and the 31st Infantry, which was all
American troops, the only all-American outfit out there.
The rest of the units were Filipino-American officers, but
Filipino soldiers. The 45th, which I was in, was the best
outfit by far, largely because we had a hell of a fine commander, Doyle. He'd been in the Army for years, and
there wasn't a thing he didn't know about warfare. He
never missed a day out there because of sickness or anything else. I got to be very fond of him.

The medical officers were assigned to units, as follows: You have three battalions in a regiment, and you
have a regimental surgeon, you have an assistant regimental surgeon, and you have two surgeons for each battalion, a surgeon and his assistant. I had been 2d Battalion
surgeon and then Doyle moved me up to regimental surgeon, so I ended up as 45th regimental surgeon. Basi-
cally the regimental surgeon is responsible for the care
and evacuation of all the sickness and injuries that occur
in the regiment. He works directly with the commanding officer of the regiment and has under him all of the
battalion surgeons. The headquarters is where the C.O.
is; he gets information directly from the battalions as to
what the problems are regarding sickness, injuries, and
wounds in the fields. As a regimental surgeon you can

take action to solve the problems. So you have to be near the regiment headquarters.

There were two hospitals set up on Bataan; they were just set up in the open in the jungle. There was no cover. They had some beds and they were just strung out there in the jungle. Hospital #1 was under the command of Col. James W. Duckworth, and hospital #2 was under Lt. Col. James O. Gillespie. The Japs bombed hospital #1 twice. I was there the first time. I'd been discharged and was walking to a staff car that was waiting to take me back to the front to my unit when they came over, bombing the hospital. Afterward I said to my friend Fred Black, who was there, "I'm going back to the front where it's safer." I wanted to get the hell out of there.

Out in the field on Bataan we didn't have any tents; we slept on the ground. But as a doctor I had litters, and I'd sleep on a litter and I'd use the leather belt that held the sidearms for a pillow. It wasn't too comfortable. We had mosquito nets but you didn't have time to put them up. We'd only sleep a few hours a night.

Bataan is a jungle and Jap sharpshooters would be up in these trees and they'd wear all black clothes and then these tennis shoes. They'd tie themselves up there; they'd have a bag of rice, and they'd stay up there for several days. And if you were walking along the trail, they'd take a shot at you. We had a number of men killed that way. But Colonel Doyle, he'd take his machine guns, and if there was a tree, a good-sized tree, that's the kind of tree the Jap would use, he'd point a machine gun and just take it out on the tree and the Jap would fall down to the ground. He'd nail the Jap that way.

As far as food goes, when the war started in December, we had three meals a day, and we were out in the open; we were hungry as can be. And then, as I mentioned, I was near a stream and I used to go over there swimming, at least once a day, sometimes twice. It was a beautiful spring. But then at the beginning of January, they cut the food rations in half. They were running out of food. They had food there for twenty thousand people; they expected that twenty thousand troops would be there, and they had enough for six months, but a hundred thousand people! The whole Philippine army went to Bataan. So they had to immediately start rationing food. We'd get breakfast, and no lunch, and then a little supper. We all lost weight rapidly. I started out at about 150–155 pounds; by the fall of Bataan at the beginning of April, I was down to 137 pounds, and a lot of that was edema, fluid that collects around your ankles (because of beriberi).

We also developed a peripheral neuritis. One day three or four of us were sitting around, and I said I couldn't feel anything in my feet. Colonel Smith said, "I haven't been able to feel anything up to my knees for a couple of weeks now." It's a strange feeling when you walk along and you can't feel the ground. It's not a very pleasant feeling either. The neuritis was from the beriberi. There are two kinds of beriberi, wet and dry. One will often turn into the other. With wet beriberi you have the edema; with dry, the peripheral neuritis.

We also rapidly developed night blindness. It's due to lack of vitamin A. You don't realize it, but in the dark you see quite a bit ordinarily, but with night blindness you see nothing. You're blind, absolutely blind, and you can't see anything. You can't see your hand in front of you.

After awhile, when we were out of everything in the field, I knew they had supplies at hospital #1, and I knew the sergeant in charge of the food there, so I went to him. I said, "We're starved out there on the front lines. Can you get me some food?" He said, "Yeah, come with me to the mess hall storeroom. Pick out whatever you want, all you can carry." Then he gave me a big can of alcohol, it was a gallon of pure alcohol, and he said, "You can mix that with some sort of juice. All you need is about an ounce of that stuff, and a couple of ounces of juice." He said the alcohol you've got to be careful with, it's twice as strong as whiskey. And so I took that back to my unit with me, and this captain, name was Doolin, who was my assistant, and I mixed up a couple of drinks. There were a few bushes between us and Colonel Smith, but he smelled that alcohol right away. So he comes around for a visit to wish us good-evening. I had just finished mixing this stuff in our canteens, and I stuck it down right under some litters, and Doolin stuck his down so you couldn't see it either. Smith sat there for about an hour waiting for us to give him a drink, but we never offered and he never asked for any, so finally he gave up and went back.

Smith had an adjutant by the name of Biedenstein. They had a telephone line with wire connection to the four companies. Beidenstein would fall asleep with the microphone open, and in his dreams he'd say, "Smith, Attack immediately!" "Jones! Attack! Attack!" Then you'd finally wake him up. But they would hear him over the radio system that was connected to the four companies. Sometimes the company commanders thought these were orders.

Biedenstein never knew north from south or east or west. He never knew where he was. Sometimes he would call for artillery fire, for example, and he'd say, "Send it northeast!" Then Smith would correct him: "No! for God's sake, that'll land right here, tell them to send it southwest." But often they had already started firing and they actually killed some of our men that way. The shells would drop close to us before Smith would have a chance to cancel Biedenstein's order. Biedenstein was a good friend of mine, but not too smart when it came to directions. Part of the problem was that they'd never been in Bataan before. I'd been in Bataan on maneuvers many times and I knew Bataan. Most of them, it was their first time there, and they never knew where the hell they were.

One night Biedenstein was driving and Smith and I were sitting in the back. Smith said, "Stop the car for a minute. I want to get out and take a leak here." So he stepped out of the car and it happened to be we were right next to a hell of a cliff, so when Smith stepped out of the car, you could hear him drop. I mean, he just dropped; we could count to about ten before we heard him hit. Finally he managed to climb back up, and he got back in the car, but he never said a word.

Smith survived Bataan and he survived prison camp too. After the war I ran into an officer I knew stationed at Fort Sill, Oklahoma, and I described Smith to him. I said, "Did you ever run into a Ross Smith?" If an officer has been a prisoner of war, you can tell by the ribbons he had. He said, yes, Smith was always in the bar. He said from the time the bar opened to the time it closed, he was always sitting there, drinking. I said that sounds like Smith. He didn't live that long, only a couple of years. Smith was a hell of a good commander, though, and a hell of a smart guy. He was a real boozer before the war started—and I guess after—but on Bataan when we couldn't get any liquor, he sobered up and turned out to be a fine commander. His unit was one of the best out there.

We had a couple of staff cars that the chaplain, Dick Carburry, and I got ahold of. The commanding officer, Doyle, had a staff car and he gave the other one to the chaplain and me. When you say chaplain, you think of a kind of holy individual, but this Carburry, he'd been an all-Western halfback at Oregon. His brother was one of the famous players of Notre Dame. Carburry was always writing letters to the nurses. They were all crazy about him. He was very handsome, and he would write them letters, telling them they're supposed to say a certain number of prayers every day. One day he said to me, "You know, I haven't said any of those prayers for about a month."

Fred Black, a good friend of mine, was in charge of the Jap prisoners. We took a few Jap prisoners on Bataan. He treated them very well. When we were going to leave Bataan, he asked the leader of the Japs to give him a little note of appreciation. He thought it would stand him in good stead because he knew we were going to be captured. So the Jap wrote out this thing and later on Black showed it to a Filipino who spoke Japanese, and he said, "You better destroy that. If you ever showed that to a Jap he'd take you right out and shoot you." Black was later lost on one of the prison ships.

One time the Philippine Scouts had some Jap prisoners. They were supposed to take them up to a prison camp near the hospital. But when they got there they didn't have any. They were asked where the prisoners were. They said, "They all tried to escape and we shot them." Actually, they had just lined them up and shot them.

Bataan was one of the worst places in the world for mosquitoes and for malaria. To treat it, we gave quinine as a prophylactic; we gave the troops ten grains of quinine daily—till the quinine ran out. As soon as it did we began to come down with malaria cases. By the time of the fall of Bataan, hospital #2 had over a thousand cases of malaria. It was quite a factor really in the fall of Bataan. Between malaria and the lack of food, that's what caused the surrender.

We saw quite a few bullet wounds, of course. But it was dark, you know, lots of it was at night. One night, they called me: "A fellow has been hit here." So I went up and I felt his shoulder and he had no head there. His head had been shot away.

It was a little dangerous walking around there at night, because the Filipinos were very excitable, and they would fire at anything that moved; so if you got up at night, you had to make some noise, to keep the Filipinos from shooting you. They killed a couple of Americans walking down one path—Trail 8, it was called. One time we were camped for the night in a kind of circle and this Jap officer came walking along into the middle of it. About four of our machine guns hit him and, Jeez, he was cut to pieces. Roosevelt wanted a samurai sword, so they got this guy's sword and sent it to him.

There was one occasion where I got cut off from my unit. The battalion front was up about twenty miles above the defense line. Colonel Smith was up in front leading the battalion, and I, the medical officer, usually stayed at the back, and I was at the back on this occasion. The unit was moving back. Colonel Smith had been appointed as head of this so-called "shell." I didn't know it at the time, but a "shell" is a suicide operation. Smith had three companies under him and their job was to hold the Japs at bay while the main unit of the U.S. forces moved back. They were making a major change in position, moving back to the second defense line. I volunteered to go with them. We were going single file through the jungle with Colonel Smith leading the group. We all had night blindness and we had to stick close to the person in front. In fact, we all put a white handkerchief hanging on our backs, so you could see the person in front of you.

When they retreated, they used to stop periodically to give the men a rest period. While we were marching back along after Smith, we stopped for a rest period. Well, I thought it was a little long; usually it was about a ten-minute period, but it must have been about fifteen minutes, and I thought, "Jesus, what's happened here?" So I went forward and found that the main unit had gone on ahead. I had about twenty soldiers there, who were still sleeping on the ground. I woke them up and told them to wait there, but not to go back to sleep again. Then I ran up ahead, passing these troops in single file, and soon came to a break. There were only about eight or ten men ahead of me, and then there was nothing. What had happened was they had fallen asleep and hadn't followed the line.

I realized I had to find the main unit quickly. There were Japs all over the place. They fired flares sort of like firecrackers up in the air to keep track of each other, and you'd see those going off. Any time you would see one of these things going up, you knew there were Japs there. There were a lot of them within ten yards or so of me, so I ran forward. There were two paths. I didn't know which one Smith had gone down. I ran down one of the paths, as fast as I could, and it was a dead end; I decided that they hadn't gone down that one. So I had to come back and take the other one. I ran back to the troops that I had told to wait, and I told them to follow me. We went down the second path and finally caught up to the main unit. Then I stopped the last men and I said, "Stop the column. Stop the troops! Pass the word!" They repeated that all the way up to Smith. Finally I caught up with Smith, and he said, "What the hell do you want to stop us for?" I said, "I lost the unit. There was a break back there and I didn't know where the hell you were going. I've got a group back here. We didn't know how to get out of here." He said, "Okay," and we started following him again.

Then we came to a big bunch of bamboo trees, and a Filipino said, "I can take you through this grove." The trees were so close together you could hardly get by. You had to push the trees apart to get through, because you were carrying a knapsack. He took us in there and got us all twisted up in it. And the Japs had set up machine guns, up on a little hill, and started firing into us. Fortunately, there was a young officer, a temporary captain, originally from VMI [Virginia Military Institute] and a hell of a nice young guy—we got to be quite good friends. He said, "I think I can get out of this mess." So he got ahead of the unit, and everybody followed him, and we got out.

After we got out of the bamboo thicket, we started down on the road leading to the bay. That's what we had wanted to do: go back to the road down the coast of Bataan. We were trying to get back to the main force, Doyle's regiment. We had to get back to our main line of defense. We were way up ahead of them, and we were going down this road toward the bay. We had a choice of one of two ways: either cut through the jungle and go down and hit our main line of resistance, or we could go back toward the Jap lines and then circle around, and come back to the main road. Jap troops were coming at us, so the colonel called the company commanders to vote. There were four of them; two wanted to go this way and two wanted to go the other way. He asked me how I wanted to vote, and I said, "We want to go right back around this way toward the Japs and then circle around that way." It's close to the ocean there. The idea was to go down there and then follow the road down toward Mariveles. So that's the way we went. We knew there were Japs between us and the bay. But the other way was through the jungle. So we started down this road, and then we saw a group of soldiers coming toward us. I thought they were Japs. I told the unit I was with to spread out, and I soon found that they weren't—they were Filipinos.

Then we ran into a Jap machine gun up on a little hill ahead of us. We hit the ground and I could hear the bullets spattering down right next to me. I thought, well, if he moves his gun he's going to get us all, but if he comes back the same way he went down then we're safe. Well, he went back the same way, so that we heard the bullets come back and hit the ground right next to us. They couldn't have missed us by more than six inches.

So we managed to get beyond him, but several men had been left behind. I finally hit the main road, which runs along a valley that divides Bataan into two parts, with Bagac at one end of it and Orion at the other. I found Colonel Doyle standing in the middle of the road, and I went up to him and I told him what had happened. I said, "Let's go back—we've left about ten men behind here." Also on the road there was a tank unit from Janesville, Wisconsin, and I told this tank commander, who was a general, about the men left behind. I said, "General, could you take a few tanks and go back and pick up these men?" He said, "I can't move in the day-time. It's daytime now. The only time we can move is at night. The Japs will bomb the hell out of us." So we had to leave them back there. The rest of us proceeded down the trail toward the bay. We went several miles, until we got down to Mariveles, which was the jumping-off point to Corregidor.

I received the DSC [Distinguished Service Cross] for an incident that occurred during this engagement. Dick Carbury, the chaplain, was right there with me. It was while we were under heavy machine-gun fire. I had acci-dentally left my medical bag behind. The Japs were about ten yards away, but if you kept low the bullets would miss you, going right over your head. I ducked down and ran forward and grabbed my medical bag, and then we went back up this trail around them and got out of their range. Carburry was very impressed with that. When he got back he told the chief nurse. They wrote it up and decided to make the recommendation for the medal. MacArthur used medals as incentives. He'd promise a person if they would accomplish a certain mission for him, he'd give them a DSC. Once he sent a general on a very dangerous mission back to the Philippines. He said, "If you accomplish this mission, I'll give you the DSC. If you don't accomplish it, leave your body up there." He also used medals for political purposes. He realized that for each person that received a medal there would be good publicity in the hometown papers.

I learned about the Distinguished Service Cross after I had just come back from a walk. They said they were recommending me for the Congressional Medal of Honor. Well, it didn't mean anything to me at that time. Smith said, "You know, the President personally will give you the medal. It's a hell of a big ceremony. They'll send you down to Washington. It'll be a big affair."

I heard Smith make the recommendation. They had a walkie-talkie connected to headquarters on Corregidor. Doyle was talking to MacArthur's office. I was standing right next to them and I could hear what they were saying. They told Doyle, "The President wants to give the Congressional Medal. Write up a little story about somebody, and send it over and we'll wire it back to the U.S." So Doyle wrote up my story and sent it on to Corregidor. Then they wanted to know, "Has this man been injured or anything?" He said no. "Well," they said, "pick somebody else then, because it's the policy to give the Congressional Medal to somebody that's been injured by a combat wound. Since he's not, we can't give him the

Congressional Medal. We'll give him the DSC instead. That's nothing to be ashamed of. We'll keep this same write-up and use it for the DSC." MacArthur personally approved it. He asked just one question. He said, "Where did it occur?" He wanted to make sure it had taken place in an important area. When he learned it had, he approved it.

Later on, when we'd gotten over to Corregidor, Colonel Doyle said, "I'm recommending you all for the DSC." They sent it in, but Wainwright's staff—Wainwright was in command by this time—didn't have the authority to give out a DSC. They said the best they could give is a Silver Star. So I got a Silver Star there. Later on, on Corregidor, I got recommended for a Bronze Star. I was then with the 92d Coast Artillery, and the most the colonel of that unit could recommend was a Bronze Star. So he recommended me for a Bronze Star, and the Secretary of the Army gave the Bronze Star to everybody that was on Bataan, so I got two Bronze Stars there, and then I got a third one—the adjutant for the 45th also recommended me for a Bronze Star—and then there was a fourth recommendation, so I ended up with four Bronze Stars. I had one Distinguished Service Cross, one Silver Star, four Bronze Stars, and two Army Commendation Medals.

The real war took place on Bataan. Once Bataan fell, it was just a matter of time till Corregidor would go. The fighting on Bataan was tough. It was vicious. Some of it was hand-to-hand fighting with bayonets. They used to say:

> We're the battling bastards of Bataan
> No mother, no father, no Uncle Sam.

We managed to leave Bataan just before it fell and just before the infamous Death March. We got over to

Corregidor. Colonel Doyle, the regimental commander, made a famous remark—and I heard him say it—"We don't seem to take many prisoners." They had spies all over the place, and so some Filipino picked it up. And the next day the main Manila paper was reporting: "Colonel Doyle says that the 45th Infantry won't take prisoners. They're going to murder them all." So then the Japs said, "When we get Doyle we're going to hang him from the nearest tree. Bataan is going to fall very shortly and as soon as it does, we'll get Doyle." MacArthur was in Australia, but he was still in command of the Philippines, and he sent word to get Doyle out of there. He knew Doyle had done a hell of a fine job, and Doyle was a good friend of his and he wanted them to save Doyle.

I was with Colonel Doyle when we got the word to leave. We were quite a way from the ship, which was landing at Mariveles. We were way up north and the road was crowded, just full of army cars and tanks. On our way down Doyle had to stop in at the headquarters for the Philippine division to see what was going on. We waited for him on the road. He was in for quite a while and when he came out he said, "The flag goes up at six o'clock tomorrow morning." In other words, they were surrendering. Then he said, "They want to get me out of here. I don't know why but they've got orders from MacArthur to get me out of here. They want me to make the boat leaving Mariveles at six o'clock in the morning. He told me to be sure and make that boat, to get on it and get the hell out of here."

Meanwhile they had started blowing up the ammunition. There were some awful explosions. They didn't want the Japs to get all the ammunition they had on Bataan. During these explosions the ground suddenly started moving and it knocked us off our feet. I fell down and was lying next to this Filipino, and he said, "Oh, that's nothing, it's just an earthquake." So we had an earthquake then, too, on top of everything else. They had a lot of earthquakes out there.

So we were about twenty-five miles away from Mariveles, trying to get down there by 6 A.M. It was just thick with troops, and trucks, and guns. We started down. We had two staff cars. Doyle wanted to get the whole regiment out too, get them to Corregidor. They wanted to get at least a battalion out to Corregidor if they possibly could. Doyle sent one staff car back to the unit, which was just a short distance away, and told them to tell the troops to get on vehicles, whatever they could—any kind at all, just get on, hang on, to get down in a hurry. Then Doyle said, "We'll go ahead in this staff car; we'll hold the ship up until you get there." We started off, and we had a dental officer with us. Actually there was a Filipino that was going too—sitting in the front seat. The dental officer came to me and he said, "Let that Filipino, let him stay. When this place falls, they're not going to bother the Filipinos any, but you know what they'll do to the Americans."

I told the Filipino to get out and gave the place to the dental officer. And he did a hell of a good job of clearing the way. I'd been up for about two to three nights and was just half dead. In the back seat I slept most of the way, but this dental officer he would just get out of the car, push, and clear whatever was blocking traffic. Then a messenger came along and yelled, "Message for Colonel Doyle! Message for Colonel Doyle!" And Doyle said, "Here, over here." He took it and showed it to me. The message read, "A major naval engagement is going on off Southern point," and it went on to tell about the naval battle, and then at the bottom it ordered, "Doyle, Make the Boat!" "What do you think of this?" he asked. "Well, Jesus," I said, "it looks like they're having a big naval battle." Doyle answered, "That's all artifice; that means nothing. There's only one thing in that message that means anything and that's the last sentence, 'Doyle, Make the Boat!' " He said, "They want to get me out of here apparently."

We started off again, and we finally got to the boat. It was supposed to have left at six o'clock, and we were late, but the captain kept it waiting for us. Doyle said, "We'll go on ahead and hold the boat up until the troops get here."[20] Along with me was Dick Carburry, the chaplain. When we got there, the captain met us up on the deck. Then up came the gangplank, and off the boat went. There were about five or six of us on board. It couldn't wait any longer because it couldn't move in daylight or it would get bombed. We left just as the formal surrender of Bataan began. We were probably the last boat to leave.

And so we went to Corregidor; that was a dangerous trip. The whole area was mined. You had to know what you were doing, you couldn't just go straight; you had to go zigzagging around. If you hit one of those mines, you'd get blown to hell and gone. So when we got to Corregidor, we went up and reported to Wainwright, and then Wainwright said to Doyle, "There's a submarine leaving immediately; you're to be on that submarine to get out of here. MacArthur has ordered you out." So Doyle left on the submarine, the last submarine to leave. The submarine commanders said it was awfully dangerous after that. Jap ships were dropping depth bombs. So the rest of us sat there on Corregidor until the Japs landed and Wainwright surrendered.

Doyle and I got on fine. I liked him; I admired him, and I corresponded with him after the war; we used to write back and forth. He was criticized unjustly for the fact that he'd gotten out. But MacArthur wanted him out, and he had no choice because MacArthur was in command. Doyle was criticized a lot, because they thought that he had left his troops and saved himself, and the hell with them. That wasn't true at all; he wanted to go back. As a matter of fact, when we got to Corregidor, he said to Carburry and me, "It looks awful for me to be here and the troops there." But he added, "I had no control over that at all." "

Notes

1. Richard C. Mallonée, *The Naked Flagpole: Battle for Bataan*, ed. Richard C. Mallonée II (San Rafael, CA: Presidio, 1980), 84.
2. Spector, *Eagle against the Sun*, 135. Further details about the medical situation on Bataan, Corregidor, and in the POW camps may be found in Colonel Wibb E. Cooper et al., "Medical Department Activities in the Philippines from 1941 to 6 May 1942, and Including Medical Activities in Japanese Prisoner of War Camps," unpublished manuscript, 1946, Center of Military History, Washington, DC. Major William N. Donovan was one of the authors of this report.
3. Toland, *But Not in Shame*, 163.
4. Louis Morton, *The Fall of the Philippines* (Washington, DC: Department of the Army, 1953), 277.
5. Ibid., 287.
6. Ibid., 288.
7. Toland, *But Not in Shame*, 70.
8. Spector, *Eagle against the Sun*, 116.
9. Lt. Gen. E. M. Flanagan, Jr., *Corregidor: The Rock Force Assault* (Novato, CA: Presidio, 1981), 43.
10. Morton, *Fall of the Philippines*, 315.
11. Ibid.
12. Ibid., 316.
13. Ibid., 324.
14. D. Clayton James, *The Years of MacArthur*, vol. 2, *1941–1942* (Boston: Houghton Mifflin, 1975), 60.
15. Morton, *Fall of the Philippines*, 323–24.
16. Douglas MacArthur, *Reminiscences* (New York: McGraw-Hill, 1964), 132.
17. Morton, *Fall of the Philippines*, 437.
18. Ibid., 443.
19. Douglas MacArthur statement, February 19, 1945, as cited in *Heroes of Bataan, Corregidor, and Northern Luzon*, 2d ed., eds.

Marcus Griffin and Eva Jane Matson (Las Cruces, NM: Yucca Tree, 1989), frontispiece.

20. In hopes of saving at least one division, MacArthur had ordered the 45th to evacuate to Corregidor, but the troops did not make it to Mariveles in time. See Donald J. Young, *The Battle of Bataan* (Jefferson, NC: McFarland, 1992), 283, 319.

3

Corregidor

CORREGIDOR, A 2.75-SQUARE-MILE island of volcanic rock, controls the entrance to Manila Bay. So long as the Americans held Corregidor the Japanese could not use Manila, which was about thirty miles away, as a naval base. Along with three other islands in Manila Bay—Caballo (Fort Hughes), El Fraile (Fort Drum), and Carabao (Fort Frank)—Corregidor (Fort Mills) formed a formidable armed fortress.

Called "the Rock," Corregidor was a long, narrow strip of land shaped like a tadpole stretching five miles from east to west and one-and-a-half miles from north to south. The defenses on Corregidor were characterized by a unique and elaborate tunnel system called the Malinta Tunnel, which had been dug by the Army Corps of Engineers before the war. The main tunnel was 1,450 feet long and 30 feet wide with an arched ceiling rising to a height of 20 feet. An electric railroad ran the length of the tunnel. There were twenty-five lateral wings, each of a length of about 400 feet. Of these, twelve wings formed the hospital complex, which was situated to the northeast of the main tunnel. By the time of the fall of Corregidor, the 1,000-bed hospital was full. There were three entrances to the tunnel, two to the main tunnel and one to the hospital area. The tunnels were constructed of reinforced concrete and ventilated with a system of fans. Corregidor was armed with powerful 12-inch guns, as well as antiaircraft batteries; Fort Drum had two even more massive 14-inch guns.

Captain Donovan was attached to the 92d Coast Artillery Battalion (PS) under the command of Colonel Biggs; the unit was stationed "topside" toward the tail end of the island on the coast facing Bataan, which was about two-and-a-half miles away. By the end of the siege, however, his unit had been relocated inside the tunnel.

At the time of the surrender of U.S. forces on Bataan on April 9, there were approximately 11,500 U.S. and Filipino troops on Corregidor. The final siege of the island lasted from April 9 until May 6, when (recently promoted) Lt. Gen. Jonathan Wainwright, who had succeeded MacArthur as commander-in-chief, surrendered his forces, which included approximately 8,700 Americans, to the Japanese.

By mid-February it had become apparent to the American command that, as one historian put it, "the Philippines had been . . . irrevocably written off, their only value now as a symbol of last-ditch resistance."[1] On February 10, MacArthur received a cable from Roosevelt: "IT IS MANDATORY," it read, "THAT THERE BE ESTABLISHED ONCE AND FOR ALL IN THE MINDS OF ALL PEOPLES COMPLETE EVIDENCE THAT THE AMERICAN DETERMINATION AND INDOMITABLE WILL TO WIN CARRIES DOWN TO THE LAST UNIT."[2] Bataan and Corregidor were to provide that evidence.

During the one-month siege the forces on Corregidor were subjected to intense air and artillery bombardments, one of the most concentrated of the war. On May 4 alone, for example, an estimated sixteen thousand Japanese shells fell on the island.[3] By the end of the siege what had been a pleasant, well-shaded island with lush dense vegetation and grass was a pile of rubble, ash, and charred tree stumps. According to Hanson Baldwin in the *New York*

Times, "by May 5, Corregidor [had been] blasted, burned and scarred beyond recognition."[4]

General MacArthur's headquarters was located in the tunnel until he was ordered by President Roosevelt on February 22 to remove to Australia, where he was to organize the Pacific command for the recapture of the Philippines and the ultimate defeat of Japan. On March 11, MacArthur, his family, and several staff officers departed on four PT-boats. As he looked back on Corregidor, MacArthur later reminisced, "gone was the vivid green foliage, with the trees, shrubs, and flowers. Gone were the buildings, the sheds, every growing thing. The hail of relentless bombardment had devastated, burned, and blasted. Ugly dark scars marked smouldering paths where the fire had raged from one end of the island to the other."[5]

MacArthur's entourage reached the north coast of Mindanao early on March 13, whence they were to fly to Australia. MacArthur refused, however, to leave on the plane supplied because he thought it in poor condition and poorly equipped. He was then sent two B-17s, with experienced pilots, which departed on March 17, arriving several hours later near Darwin, Australia. The next day, in Adelaide, MacArthur made his memorable remark to the press: "I shall return." Shortly thereafter he learned that the American forces in Australia numbered only twenty-five thousand, which was shockingly fewer than he had anticipated, making it apparent that his return would be much later than he had planned.

On May 3, when it became clear that his forces could not hold out much longer, General Wainwright cabled MacArthur: "SITUATION HERE IS FAST BECOMING DESPERATE."[6] In return he received a telegram dated May 5 from Roosevelt, commending him and his forces for their heroic stand: "IN SPITE OF ALL THE HANDICAPS OF COMPLETE

ISOLATION YOU HAVE GIVEN THE WORLD A SHINING EXAMPLE OF PATRIOTIC FORTITUDE AND SELF-SACRIFICE," noting that their example would inspire troops elsewhere, as well as shipyard and munitions workers on the home front, to "REDOUBLE THEIR EFFORTS. . . . YOU AND YOUR DEVOTED

Japanese news photo of the Corregidor surrender, May 6, 1942, at the mouth of the Malinta Tunnel. *National Archives*

FOLLOWERS HAVE BECOME THE LIVING SYMBOL OF OUR WAR AIMS AND THE GUARANTEE OF VICTORY."[7]

After the Japanese landed on Corregidor, and with their tanks approaching the tunnel, Wainwright surrendered on May 6. Just before, he cabled a last message to Roosevelt: "WITH BROKEN HEART AND HEAD BOWED IN SADNESS BUT NOT IN SHAME . . . WITH PROFOUND REGRET AND WITH CONTINUED PRIDE IN MY GALLANT MEN, I GO TO MEET THE JAPANESE COMMANDER. GOOD-BYE, MR. PRESIDENT."[8]

Meanwhile, as the surrender negotiations began, around noon on the 6th, an army radio operator in the tunnel, Corporal Irving Strobing, continued transmitting informally. Captain Donovan was next to him as he sent out final good-byes from Corregidor.

When, shortly thereafter, MacArthur learned of the fall of Corregidor, he said, "Corregidor needs no comment from me. . . . It has scrolled its own epitaph on enemy tablets. But through the bloody haze of its last reverberating shot, I shall always seem to see a vision of grim, gaunt, ghastly men, still unafraid."[9]

"Whhen we got to Corregidor, we reported first to General Jonathan Wainwright, the commanding officer, and then to the medical commander, Col. Wibb Cooper, who assigned us out to the field. He sent my friend John Breslin, a doctor, one place and sent me another. He put us on this Jeep saying, "The Jeep will take you where you're going." He meant the driver, of course. He said, "The Jeep knows the road," and "You'll be stationed up there." So we got in the Jeep. It was already dark, and since we had night blindness, we couldn't see a goddamn thing. This guy, the driver, took me up there to my new assignment and dropped me off. He said, "Here's where you're going to be stationed. Get off here." I got off and he left, and there I was, standing in the middle of nowhere. I couldn't see a thing. The tunnel was about a mile away.

A Colonel Biggs was in charge of my new unit, the 92d Coast Artillery. He saw them drop me off and called to me. "Come on over here!" he hollered. So I followed his voice and finally reached him. He said, "You're coming to a hot place here. My adjutant had his arm shot off today. The medical officer up here just went crazy—the one that you're replacing, he went crazy today. They've got him locked up down in the tunnel." So that was my greeting to this new job.

Biggs came to a sad end, as it turned out. He came from someplace down in central Illinois. He used to spend his time figuring out what medal he would get. He said if he could get a DSC he'd run for Senate after the war, and if he could only get a Silver Star he'd run for the House of Representatives. But he died a horrible death after he was caught trying to escape. He wanted me to escape too, with him, but I said, "No, they'll murder you if they catch you." He said he knew where there was a boat hidden on Corregidor, and he wanted to take that boat over to the mainland, Luzon, finally working south to Australia. But I didn't like the idea. So Biggs decided to take off by himself, but he was caught. He was crawling along in a trench, and there was a Jap guard up above, who leaked on him. And he said, "For God's sake, stop that!" and that was the end of his escape. They tied him to a post and what they didn't do to him. For two or three days they just beat him, they smashed his face in, they broke his jaw. He was crying out, "For God's sake, shoot me!" After a few days they finally shot him.

Corregidor is an island about five miles long, a mile and a half wide, and about a thousand feet high. They called it "the Rock." The Corps of Engineers had built a tunnel right straight through the middle of it. It was about twenty to thirty yards wide and had a train track running the length of it. It was also "air conditioned." You could live in it. Then they had these laterals off the main tunnel; one was a medical wing. It had a thousand beds, which were all filled before the war was over.

There are four islands in Manila Bay, including Corregidor, Fort Hughes, and Fort Drum. Drum had big 14-inch guns, which is a hell of a large gun. When we got to Corregidor, these 14-inch guns began firing over to Bataan and they killed a hell of a pile of Japs there. They called them flying boxcars. They're immense shells and you can see them go, but they don't go so fast. They sort of sail along and it makes a hell of a "Voom-voom!"

Meanwhile the Japs were bombing Corregidor. More bombs fell on Corregidor per square foot than any other place in history, I believe. The guns we had on Corregidor would only go up about twenty thousand feet. The Japs would fly at about twenty-two thousand feet. Then finally we got some new shells that would go up to about twenty-four thousand feet. The Japs that were flying over Corregidor that day got a rude awakening. We shot down a whole fleet of them, but the communiqué that they put out was pure bunk, saying that we shot down only about forty planes that day, when actually it was about seventy. If they ever added up all the Jap planes we shot down over Corregidor, it must have been a thousand or two.

On several occasions the bombs landed close to us. Once we were sleeping in our hammocks when heavy shelling started in. I said to my friend, "It's getting a little close here," and I walked over to a little dugout, about eight feet deep, that was nearby. I decided to stay there until the shelling subsided; shortly thereafter my friend joined me. About five minutes later a shell landed right where we had been and blew up his hammock. There were two tunnel entrances facing Bataan, and people used to sit outside of the entrances at night and smoke. The Japs started sending shells over one night from Bataan and killed a bunch of people sitting at the entrance. Another time I was inside the tunnel when a bomb landed right at the entrance. Suddenly it became dark, and I thought sure in hell I was going to be buried in the tunnel. But when I got up to the entrance, I found there was room enough to get out.

Breslin and I used to go down there to the Engineers' section of the tunnel, because they had plenty of food stored there; they even had pancakes for breakfast. On Bataan we had been without food sometimes for two or three days at a time, and so on Corregidor we'd go down there in the tunnel and eat. Jeez, the food was wonderful.

There was a captain there who was sort of in charge of food supplies. He was regular army, under a major who was reserve. But the major turned over the job to this captain. The captain said that they were never going to take him to Japan. Later on, however, they took that whole group from Corregidor, including him, and put them on a ship bound for Japan. The ship traveled only at night because during the daytime they could get bombed by American bombers. (The Japs didn't identify them as prison ships.) So this ship was traveling north not far from the coast, probably about a couple of hundred yards, and one night the captain dove over the side. The Japs saw it and machine-gunned him in the water, and that was the end of him.

There was an Indian there who was also a priest. He needed an altar boy to say Mass. I knew how to be an altar boy from my days at St. Raphael's in Madison, and so I used to serve Mass with him. He knew a lot about protecting himself and he taught me some useful things, such as, "never walk so you can see your own shadow" and "never have a lit cigarette in your hand."

General MacArthur was in command there until he was evacuated. He had been named commander-in-chief along about July in 1941, at which time he had wanted to fight the Japs when they landed at Lingayen Beach. But he'd had to change the plan, as I mentioned. He was a skillful propagandist. For example, when the Japs attacked Manila, they didn't bomb the city, although MacArthur put out that they did. They did bomb the port area—and one bomb accidentally fell on a church. MacArthur made a big deal out of it, let out to the press that they were bombing churches and everything else in the city.

When Wainwright took over, he took a very conciliatory attitude toward the Japs, and whatever they did he'd say they didn't mean to do it. When they bombed hospital #1 over in Bataan, Wainwright came out and said he thought they did it by mistake, that they were aiming at something else, which was pure bunk. I didn't have much respect for Wainwright. MacArthur was so far superior, there was no comparison. MacArthur was a brilliant man; Wainwright wasn't. Wainwright was pretty much loaded with booze all day long. MacArthur never drank. They offered him a drink once. He said, "If I'm going to command these fine young men, I'm not going to be under the influence of liquor."

MacArthur was absolutely fearless. Once, on Bataan, he was walking along with a medical officer, and the Japs were taking shots at him. The Japs were in trees, and this guy that he was with said, "General, don't you think you ought to take cover, you're going to get hit." And MacArthur said, "These people—the ones that are shooting at us—are very poor shots." He said, "Their top shooting men are not here, they're at the front. These men are very incompetent. They're not going to hit us." And they didn't, either. He had a theory that the bullet that would hit him had to have the same number as his serial number. He said the Japs were never going to get him.

One time I sat across from MacArthur at breakfast. When I was on Bataan we went over to Corregidor to try to get more supplies. They were saving them over there. We never knew why. I ate at the hospital mess there, which was in the tunnel. MacArthur always ate there, and I sat across the table from him that morning for breakfast. Unlike some other commanders, MacArthur would eat exactly what the troops ate. As I say, he ate in the mess with the rest of us. Now Colonel Duckworth, for example, when we were all starving on Bataan, was eating special desserts. I happened to be there once when his cooks delivered a big apple pie to him. He was embarrassed to have me see that, so he said, "Oh, they just want to please me; I can't do anything about it." But he didn't offer me any. I know he just ate the whole thing after I left.

Later in the day on Corregidor, the time we went over for supplies, I was standing near the entrance to the tunnel with Ken Hagen and Warren Wilson, another ENT doctor, who knew MacArthur. And I saw MacArthur come walking along. I said to the others, "Here comes MacArthur. We'd better give him a good salute." But Wilson said, "No, he doesn't want any salutes. He'd be saluting all day if everybody saluted him." So we just stood at attention, and MacArthur walked by. He said, "Good evening, doctors."

MacArthur was ordered to leave Corregidor, along in February, but he didn't leave; he thought it would look bad. Then he was ordered again to leave, this time by General George Marshall—Marshall was chief of staff— and still he refused to leave. Finally he got a direct order from Roosevelt to leave, and he left on the 11th of March,

1942. The Japs had Manila Bay covered, of course; he had to break through Jap lines to get out of there. He took off on a PT-boat. The PT-boats were very fast, you know, they'd go about forty or fifty miles an hour. The Jap destroyers couldn't hit them, they were so fast. John F. Kennedy was on a PT-boat when his boat was cut in two by a Jap destroyer, and that's when he hurt his back.

On the way down to Australia, MacArthur was switched onto a lousy plane and they stopped off on one of the islands between the Philippines and Australia. The general said he wasn't interested in taking sightseeing trips. I guess that pilot has never been heard from since. MacArthur immediately wired Washington and said he wanted a good plane to go to Australia, and, of course, they immediately sent him a brand-new plane. It was a B-17. When he got to Australia, there was a general meeting him there, and MacArthur asked, "Where's the army?" The general said, "What army are you talking about?" MacArthur replied, "The army that I'm going to lead back to the Philippines."

"Here's your army." There were about ten soldiers there.

"Is that all—there's no army here?"

"No—hell, no!" the general said, "There never was—there was an army, but on its way out here, they decided not to send it. They thought it would be a waste of time, so they left you out here high and dry."

Nevertheless, on arriving in Australia, MacArthur made his famous comment to the press: "I shall return," meaning to the Philippines. He also made a dramatic comment about the "gaunt, gray ghosts of Bataan," which I know my wife, Dode, found very upsetting.

Shortly after MacArthur's evacuation, however, in early June there occurred one of the great naval battles of history, probably the greatest, the Battle of Midway. I was on Corregidor then, after the surrender. There was a radio that the Engineers had set up that got stateside broadcasts. A Jap guard was walking back and forth, and he said, "What are they talking about?" The Engineer said, "Oh, it's from Manila, some advertisement from Manila." Happily the guard couldn't understand English, because it was coming straight from Admiral Nimitz, the commander of the Pacific, after the Battle of Midway. Nimitz said, "The Japanese fleet will never again be a threat in the eastern Pacific. The remainder of the fleet war will be fought in Japanese territories." In the Battle of Midway we sank four Japanese aircraft carriers, and the Japs couldn't replace them. Not only that but they lost all of their navy pilots. So their whole fleet was just about wiped out. The Battle of Midway was a crucial battle. It turned the tide.

So Bataan fell on the 9th of April, 1942, and Corregidor went about a month later, on the 6th of May. Once Bataan fell, Corregidor was doomed. The actual surrender occurred when the Japs got a couple of tanks over to Corregidor and these tanks were heading for the tunnel. I was right near the entrance to the tunnel as they approached. We could hear them firing; they were shooting at us. When we were right in front of the tunnel, a captain next to me said, "Would you like a drink?" I thought he meant water, so I said, no, my canteen was full. But he had some whiskey. So I took a drink. That was the last highball I had for a while. Then we went down into the tunnel.

When Wainwright heard that they were going to fire into the tunnel, he said, "We can't—Put the flag up." So they put the white flag up, and they surrendered. I was standing right next to the radio station there when they made their last broadcast to America just before the Japs entered the tunnel. He said, "Our hearts are heavy," or something to that effect, "and I'm signing off for a long time." He was a professional broadcaster. There was no way, no way in the world, we could have held out any longer or evacuated the troops. We just didn't have the troops to do it.

First, they took Wainwright prisoner. He was sent up to Formosa, where they sent all the generals; they had about twenty American generals. The Japs did humiliating things to them like having them cut grass with a nail clipper. These generals would be crawling around on the ground, cutting grass with a nail clipper, a little scissors. The Japs made a joke of it. They had a rule that when you met a Jap you had to bow or salute. At the time of the surrender, Wainwright wouldn't bow to them, and so they beat him up, they really whacked him. So that was the surrender.

One incident that occurred right after the surrender was the mock execution of Captain Rose, who was caught attempting to escape. When they captured Rose, they decided they were going to execute him. They set him up in front of a firing squard and they got ready to fire. Rose just stood there. A Jap officer came in at the last minute and said, "You are very brave," and stopped the execution.

Right after we were taken prisoner on Corregidor, Jack Breslin and I decided to see if we could get some food from the Japs. We had had no food for some time. We had a thousand patients there in the hospital tunnel, and there was no food for them. So Breslin and I went to Colonel Cooper, who was the C.O., and told him that we would go up to the Japs and tell them that there was no food. Cooper and the rest were afraid to go out of the tunnel at this time. But he said, "Go ahead!" and so we went on out.

We soon discovered that if you came up to a Jap guard like you knew what you were doing, and bowed to him or saluted, and then just walked along he'd let you go. He'd think you were supposed to be there. But if you asked him anything, he'd probably hit you over the head with a gun. So Breslin and I walked up to the mouth of the tunnel and bowed to the guards and took off to the headquarters. They had machine guns all around it, so you had to walk into this row of machine guns. They weren't firing, but there were Japs behind each gun. We noticed they had a dog wandering around there. Breslin started calling to him, "Here, Tojo! Here, Tojo!" I said, "For God's sake, don't say that! That's their leader's name." Breslin said, "Well, that's the dog's name!" I replied, "That would be just as if they started calling one of our dogs 'Roosevelt.'"

Anyway, we met the guards and said we wanted to see the doctor. So they took us up to Lieutenant Kiarine, who was the doctor. In the Jap army, the doctor was a combat man; he fights there with the rest of them, but after the battle he becomes a doctor again. Kiarine was sitting there in the headquarters; he kept sharpening his saber all the time I was sitting there talking to him. He always kept his saber good and sharp. He was a pretty nice guy, really. All of a sudden, though, another Jap, a young lieutenant, came up and challenged me to a duel. With a duel you two face each other with swords and each tries to slam the sword down and crack open the other person's head. I had no desire to be a part of this duel. I knew that no matter what happened I was going to be the loser in that one, because if I killed him, they'd kill me, and if I didn't kill him, he'd kill me right off the bat anyway. He challenged me to this duel because I was an American and he was a Jap. I said, "I'm a doctor. We don't duel." Happily, Kiarine sort of backed me up, so this other guy backed off and we didn't duel.

We told Kiarine there were going to be a lot of diseases like typhoid and such, because there was no food. He thought that we were saying that there already were a lot of diseases, and he got all excited about it. He actually made a lot of arrangements to have the sick brought up out of the tunnel and get them better care. Kiarine gave Breslin and me a pass so we could go anywhere on the island. They had these individual stamps about the size of a short pencil with their names on them, and he stamped the pass with that.

Kiarine used to invite us over there for lunch. We had lunch with him several times. One time he was scheduled to leave the next day, so he invited us for lunch. After we ate he left us alone for a little while, and we noticed a little cabinet there. We looked inside and found a couple of cartons of American cigarettes. Breslin said, "They stole them from us—they really belong to us, anyway—so let's take them." We loaded ourselves up with these cigarettes. We put them under our shirts and under our pant legs and everywhere, about two cartons worth of cigarettes on the two of us. Well, then Kiarine came back and said he had these cigarettes he was going to give us as a present. So he looked for them and, of course, they were gone. He bawled the hell out of the Jap guards. He thought that they had stolen them, but the guards said that they hadn't taken them. We quickly said goodbye to him and gingerly walked away. I was afraid some of the cigarettes were going to fall out of our pants or shirts, but we finally got out of there without him noticing.

After the surrender there was an enlisted man named David Provoo who began siding up to the Japs. He spoke

Japanese and acted as an interpreter when Breslin and I went over to the Jap headquarters. He called himself some sort of a Japanese priest; he shaved his head. He was also a homosexual. When I was telling the Japs about the deplorable health conditions we were under, I asked him to intercede to see if they would improve them. But he refused to do that. When I asked him why, he said, "It doesn't suit my purposes." He was very abusive toward the Americans; he would push and shove the men around and slap them.

Provoo would send down in the tunnel for food and stuff and this Captain Burton Thompson, a veterinary officer, was then in charge of the kitchen. One time Provoo was up with the Japs and he sent down that he wanted some food. Thompson told the Jap guard that came down to go back to Provoo and tell him that the next time he saw him he would kick him so hard that he would be able to taste his boot. The Jap went back and told Provoo that, and pretty soon two guards came down and grabbed Thompson. They took him out and they shot him and killed him. The Japs told me that Provoo was the one who did the shooting.

He caused a hell of a lot of trouble there for Colonel Cooper. He began threatening him. Breslin and I went to Lieutenant Kiarine about it. We said, "We've got a traitor in our group. He's already had one officer shot and he's threatening Colonel Cooper." Provoo had said to Cooper, "You know what happened to Thompson. That's what's going to happen to you." Kiarine said, "Do you want me to have him shot?" I answered, "Hell, yes," but Breslin said, "You can't do that. If we have him shot without a trial or anything, we'll get hell after the war. Let's take him over to Cooper and see what he says." But Cooper didn't recommend doing anything. So we let it go.

Provoo was tried for treason after the war. I had to go down to testify in the trial in New York in November 1952. He was convicted of treason and of contributing to Thompson's death, but the Appeals Court threw the thing out. They said he had to be tried again, because Provoo's home wasn't New York, it was Maryland; so they were going to have to try him over again. Eventually he died anyway.[10]

At the trial of Provoo, an American sergeant came up to me and asked, "Does eating ground glass hurt you?" I answered, "Yes, it can kill you." Well, he said, when he was on Corregidor he ground up a glass and put it in Provoo's food, but he ate it and never even got a stomachache out of it. I myself had gone to the Engineers about Provoo on Corregidor to see if they could get rid of him. The Engineers had a separate place, and I thought they might be able to take care of him without the Japs seeing. They said, yes, if they could get ahold of him, there was a cliff that was about a two-hundred-foot drop down to a bunch of rocks, they could try to throw him off that. They said if I could get him outside, get him down to their area, they would take care of him. But I never was able to. Provoo, he was a real traitor."

Notes

1. Toland, *But Not in Shame*, 192.

2. Ibid.

3. John Keegan, *The Second World War* (New York: Viking, 1990), 266.

4. Hanson W. Baldwin, "Corregidor: The Full Story" (from *New York Times Magazine*, September 22, 1946), in Griffin and Matson, *Heroes of Bataan*, 53.

5. MacArthur, *Reminiscences*, 142–43.

6. Toland, *But Not in Shame*, 339.

7. Ibid., 344.

8. Ibid., 375.

9. MacArthur, *Reminiscences*, 146.

10. Accounts of William Donovan's testimony in the Provoo trial are found in "Officer Betrayal Is Laid to Provoo," *New York Times*, November 14, 1952, 9; and "U.S. Captain Executed by Japs Dominates Provoo Trial," *New York World-Telegram*, November 14, 1952, 7.

4

Bilibid and Camp #8

BILIBID WAS ONE OF SEVENTEEN Japanese prison camps for the military in the Philippines. There were also several civilian camps. It was a nineteenth-century Spanish prison that had been declared unfit for criminal inmates in 1923 and abandoned; later somewhat rehabilitated, it was re-opened by the Japanese in 1942 as a prisoner-of-war internment site.

The prison was located in Manila at the intersection of Quezon Boulevard and Azcarraga Street. It was a massive, square-shaped enclosure surrounded by twelve-foot walls that ran approximately 600 feet on each side, covering a city block. Around a central guard tower twelve barracks radiated, each of which was 120 feet long and 20 feet wide, constructed of masonry and cement with corrugated iron roofs. By early July 1942 it held approximately two thousand prisoners, mostly Americans.

Most of the prisoners who had been captured on Corregidor were transferred to Bilibid by freighter on May 24. The prison hospital patients and staff, Captain Donovan among them, remained on Corregidor another several weeks, however, before being sent to Bilibid on July 2. They arrived in Manila on July 3 around noon, and those who could walk were marched through the city—a five-mile trek—to the prison. The sick were taken by truck. There they were transferred to a 100-bed Navy hospital that had already been established in the prison.

This became the central American hospital in the Philippine prison system.

Rations in Bilibid consisted of a canteen cup three-fourths full of watery *lugao* (rice) twice daily—or, in other words, about three hundred grams of rice (dry weight) per day. This was supplemented with a soup made of local greens, with an occasional fishhead thrown in. A black market system operated, with tobacco as the currency, so that it was occasionally possible to obtain additional items, such as duck eggs.

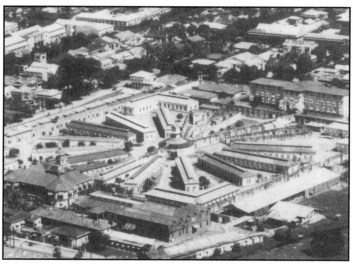

Aerial view of Bilibid Prison in Manila. *National Archives*

Red Cross supplies arrived in December of 1942 via a Swedish ship, the *Gripsholm*. While these were heavily looted and badly manhandled by the Japanese, some of the materials reached the prisoners. Another *Gripsholm* shipment arrived in November of 1943. This included personal parcels from family members. Little mail got through to the prisoners; beginning in December 1942, prisoners were allowed to send out heavily censored form cards.

Japan never ratified the 1929 Geneva Convention on the treatment of prisoners of war and rarely complied with its tenets.[1] As an officer, Captain Donovan did not have to work at heavy labor, but as a doctor he held "sick call" daily and treated other prisoners (and occasionally Japanese guards). He remained in Bilibid from early July 1942 until February 27, 1943, at which time he volunteered for duty in the port area of Manila. From then on he was held in Prison Camp #8 in Manila, which was located in a bombed-out Ford garage—the Bachrach garage—in the port area. Nearly 150 U.S. POWs were held there; their assignment was to repair Japanese vehicles. Captain Donovan served as the medical officer for these men.

Because he was outside of Bilibid and able to see some of what was happening in the city, he was able to provide information to the POWs who remained in Bilibid. It appears that the information he (and others) passed on to Commander Thomas Hayes, the hospital surgeon, was then transmitted to the Philippine underground and thence to MacArthur's returning forces. A colleague of Captain Donovan's, Dr. Willard Waterous, notes the following in his memoirs:

> Capt. Bill Donovan [was] in charge . . . with motor detail in Port Area. . . . Bill . . . was the medical officer presumably taking care of these individuals. In his case, as in the case of all work details, responsibilities were 90 percent theoretical inasmuch as no medical nor surgical supplies were available. Periodically Bill came into Bilibid presumably for consultation purposes or in an attempt to secure some sort of medication for various individuals in his outfit. As was true with all these work details, there was always some underground information and it is understandable that it was passed around assiduously but with

due discretion. Bill was a fine person and . . . had a splendid record on Bataan. He was one of the individuals of whom the Medical Department could be justly proud.[2]

Captain Donovan is also cited as an intelligence source in the memoirs of Capt. Julien M. Goodman, also a doctor who was assigned to one of the port area details. Goodman notes, "In June [1944] we made a trip to get supplies from a pier in Manila. . . . My delight in meeting Drs. Joe Van de Velde [*sic*] and Bill Donovan here was lessened only by the rumor they related. They had heard by listening to Filipino civilians working with their dock detail that Allied forces were approaching the Philippine Islands and all P.O.W.s were to be sent to Japan as soon as possible." Goodman says they had obtained their information "through the interisland underground."[3]

In September 1944, Captain Donovan was returned briefly to Bilibid, after which he was shipped to Formosa. At this point the Japanese had begun evacuating ablebodied American prisoners of war from the Philippines, sending them north to Japan and Formosa on the now infamous prison ships.

"We were taken prisoner on Corregidor, but after a few weeks they took us back to the mainland, marching us through Manila into Bilibid prison. Manila looked terrible. It was all run down. Previous to that when we were still on Corregidor, a Red Cross worker whom they had taken into Manila for some reason told us, "On each corner there was a Filipino hanging by a rope around his neck." The city looked awful—Jeez, it looked just terrible.

We had to march through Manila. They told us to get all cleaned up and dressed up, put on our best uniforms. So we did, and they marched us through the streets of Manila right into Bilibid prison, into what they used to call the "lion cages." They were just like the lion cages of a zoo. We went in there and they locked us in, and we spent the night there, sleeping on concrete. They let us out of the cages the next day. After that we were completely free to wander around. Bilibid was an immense Philippine prison, built by the Spanish in the mid-nineteenth century. It had been condemned in 1923 as unfit for habitation, but the Japs used it as a prison. They used it as sort of a central place where they would dump American prisoners. From there they would send out small details.

It was very much like any large state prison. It was a big compound with a big wall around it about twelve or maybe fourteen feet high, and on top of it were wires that had about ten thousand volts of electricity. In the front of the prison was a wooden building, which had the Jap headquarters. And on the second floor were the wires that went around the prison. They were a little lower than the second floor. Once a Jap guard decided to take a leak there and it hit this wire of ten thousand volts, and he was blown to high heaven. He was as dead as a doornail.

In prison you did your own laundry. They did issue us a little soap. That's all. You'd wash your own uniform and lay it out on the grass in the sun. I had one uniform and it got bleached almost white. Our meals consisted of rice with a little bit of soup. You'd walk through a line and they'd have a big pile of rice there and would give you a dab of rice in your mess gear. Then you'd fill your canteen cup, which held about sixteen ounces, with so-called soup. They'd throw anything in it that they had and boil it—scraps of meat or fishheads or anything like that.

Occasionally we got Red Cross boxes sent from the States. They had three different kinds of boxes: one of them was mostly meat—cans of meat; another had mostly cigarettes in it and candy and things like that (that's the one that was the most popular); and then there was one with toothpaste, etc. In a situation like that, tobacco becomes the medium of exchange. Everyone wants cigarettes. One cigarette will buy quite a bit. In fact, there was one fellow there that had a pack of cigarettes—actually he had about seven cigarettes—and he walked in among the enlisted men and traded off. He ended up with a complete, brand-new uniform that this one guy had been dragging around with him. He got that for one cigarette, and he got an expensive British shaving set (probably worth about a hundred bucks) also for a cigarette. That's what you could get for tobacco. When he got rid of these seven cigarettes that he had, he had quite a pile of stuff—toothpaste and stuff like that—that he later traded off.

Also in these boxes was a strange kind of candy. It was chocolate and looked like a Hershey bar, but if you ate a piece of it, about a quarter of a bar, you wouldn't be able to eat anything else for about two days. I don't know why but for some reason or other you just felt filled up. That was everybody's experience, and on top of that you couldn't sleep. You'd stay awake all night. I don't know what the hell they had in that candy. God knows what they put in it.

We also got parcels from our families. I got one from Dode when I was in Camp #8. Those packages were very carefully selected by our families, but they didn't seem to realize that it was terribly hot out there. For instance, my wife got a doctor to recommend some vitamin tablets, and he picked out some vitamins that were soft and covered with a kind of gelatin. Of course, in that hot climate they all melted, so I couldn't use them at all; it was just a complete waste. They also spoiled. After eating one or two of those vitamins, I developed a hell of a gastroenteritis for a couple of days. So those weren't very successful. They either made you sick or you threw them away.

Cigarettes were what everybody wanted. In addition to the American cigarettes that came in the Red Cross boxes, we were also able to buy tobacco in the city. And the Japs had some cigarettes; they used to issue us a pack every once in a while. Their tobacco was just black; the cigarettes were small, about half the size of ours. They were very thin, but a little longer than an American cigarette, and they were strong! Oh, God! I don't know what the hell was in them. They were so strong you had to just about lie down when you smoked one, or lean against something. They called them "little poison," but we smoked them.

After a while the Japs started paying us. I was paid the same as a captain in the Jap army [90 yen a month]. When they started paying us, a Jap officer came around and asked me how much I wanted to keep. We could "save" some of it in a Jap bank or keep it all. He'd already asked some of the other American officers, who had agreed to have some of their paycheck "saved" in this fashion. Captain Jones, for example, who was the commanding officer in Camp #8, said he'd keep about half of his and the rest they could save for him. So the Jap officer came to me and he said, "How much do you want?"

"I want the whole thing!" I answered.

"Don't you want to save half of it for your wife? It would be in Japan then."

"I am not worried about her," I said. "She is getting along fine."

"Okay," he said, and gave me the whole amount.

Jones, who was standing there, just about went crazy; he threw his hat on the ground and jumped on it and he yelled, "Goddamnit!" He said, "I'd like all mine, too." Finally they ended up giving everyone the whole amount. Later we had to send cards back to the States. Jones, who was on the verge of divorce from his wife, addressed his card to her care of Times Square in New York. God only knows who got that card.

After about a year and a half I finally received a letter from Dode. It must have been in late 1943 or early 1944. It had some snapshots of her and Josie. Josie was a hell of a pretty little kid and she had her all dressed up. I've carried those with me all these years. I've still got them in my pocket.

In Bilibid, you could fix up your own place and sleep wherever you wanted. Every morning you had to line up at six o'clock in the morning, and they'd take roll and be sure that no one had escaped. One morning they were short one, and we stood there from six o'clock until ten o'clock, just standing there—we had no breakfast, no nothing!—six, seven, eight, nine, ten—that's four hours just standing in one spot! And then they looked around and they found my friend Maj. John Breslin, in bed sleeping. The rest of them could have murdered him. Oh, God! Everyone was sore at him. Breslin said, "Goddamnit, I told them last night I was going to sleep in!"

Breslin had a lot of nerve. At the surrender on Corregidor the Japs took our money and then later in Bilibid they were going to return it to us. We were supposed to collect it at 11 A.M. one morning. Breslin said, "Goddamnit, they aren't going to tell me when I'm going to get my money." About 1 P.M. he went over to their office and started hollering and demanding his money. They gave it to him.

Now if someone escaped—this happened only out on detail—the next morning the whole group would know that he had. At roll call the Japs would say, "The friends of so-and-so, step forward." Whoever stepped forward would be taken over to the woods nearby and shot. They had us lined up one day, and they were searching our pockets and clothes and everything. We didn't know what the hell they were looking for. Ever so often, they would take someone over to the woods and execute him—you would hear the shot. They finally got down about two steps from us. We finally figured out that what they were looking for was Japanese money. If anybody had Japanese money they figured he'd gotten it off a dead Jap, so they would take him over and shoot him. The guy next to me in line had quite a bit of Japanese money. He didn't know what the hell to do with it, so he finally stuck it in his sock, the inside of his sock. They made him take his shoes off, but they didn't make him take his socks off. So that's how close he came to getting shot.

Later when we were being sent to Japan by ship—in the fall of 1944—before we left, they were inspecting everything we had, and I had a lot of things that I wasn't supposed to have—scissors, a scalpel, and a few things like that. You had to lay out all of your stuff on the grass for inspection. There were three Japs doing the inspection, row by row. We were near the end, and there was quite a bit of room between each row. I realized I would have time to stick my stuff up to the row ahead of us, with the stuff that had already been inspected, before they got down our row. Captain Al Poweleit, a doctor, was right next to me in line. I said to Poweleit, "Let's move ours up." So we moved our stuff up to the row that had already been inspected. They never found it.

You had to go to bed at nine o'clock. They always made you keep your abdomen covered because they had a theory that it was bad for you if your abdomen wasn't covered. And you had to sleep under a mosquito bar. They put you to bed and the lights went out and that was it. There were lots of bedbugs. If you left your arm outside the mosquito bar, it would be covered with bites the next day.

After a while I decided I wanted to move out of Bilibid. If you stayed in there for any length of time you began to get cabin fever. I wanted to get the hell out. I knew that it was bad for a person mentally to be in there. A lot of them walked around like zombies after they'd been in there a while. So I volunteered to go out—to Camp #8 in the port area. Breslin said, "What the hell do you want to go out for? We've got it perfect in here." I told him, "Hell, I'm sick of this goddamned place." So I went down to the port area in late February 1943. Captain Vandevelt, another doctor, was already there. We took care of these 150 or so prisoners, and it was much better there.

We lived in what had been a Ford garage in the port area. It was close to the ocean, although we couldn't see the water. There was a big fence around the garage. They put the officers in a separate area—there were about six of us—and we slept on cots. A bomb had hit the thing and in the middle there was a big opening, but we were covered. It was a large building. There was a big pile of debris, though, in the center where the bomb had gone off.

The prisoners worked on a detail repairing trucks, Jap trucks—that is, American trucks—stuff they had captured. Vandevelt and I were the doctors for these prisoners working in the garage. They used to sabotage the trucks. They would put water and sugar in the gas. Sugar is the worst thing you can do for a motor. The trucks would stall after a few days. The Japs never figured it out.

Eventually we were able to bribe the guards for some supplies. As I mentioned, they started paying us for some reason or other—I guess they thought they were losing the war—and there was a truck driver that used to come around. We'd give him some money and tell him to go and get us a bottle of gin. They had some good gin in a forty-two-ounce bottle called a *ganta*. It's a Spanish term. He'd come in with this *ganta* of gin for us. I was bunked next to Captain Vandevelt, and he got royally drunk on this gin. First he lay there half on the bed and half on the floor. He didn't have a stitch on. Then finally about midnight he woke up, and he went outside, about twenty feet inside of the surrounding fence. He took a chair out there and started singing "The Star Spangled Banner" and a few other things at the top of his lungs. The Japs didn't pay any attention to him. The next morning, he couldn't get up to go over to what they called *bangōday*. That's when they would line you up, but they just counted him there. They knew he was drunk. I'll tell you he had a hangover to end all hangovers.

That's the only liquor we ever had. Vandevelt and I didn't want to share it with the rest of the officers because we realized that if we did, it would be gone in one night. The two of us were separated from the rest of the group; about a half hour before they'd come back in from detail, we'd mix up a drink for ourselves. Then they'd come back and smell the liquor. Captain Jones, who was in charge, said, "Well, now, looks like we've got a couple of drunken doctors!"

Later I learned that some guy had gotten some eggs somewhere, and I had this gin. So I traded him an ounce of gin—and measured it out very carefully—for two eggs;

and he gave them to me. He had four eggs, actually. He finished his ounce of gin and he said, "Do you want to trade some more?" I said, "Yeah," and I gave him another ounce of gin for two more eggs. So I had these four eggs—duck eggs. They were good eggs. And for the next several mornings, I would build a fire and fry these eggs.

During this time there was a flood—I don't know what happened, the ocean just went up to about your waist—and the Japanese couldn't get a fire started. So the Jap guards had nothing to eat. As I say, I managed to get a little fire going, and I fixed up some toast and fried one of these eggs. I was having a nice breakfast there and this Jap guard—he was one of the worst guards we had— came over and saw me eating an egg and toast. He said, "You're a prisoner here and you're having a good breakfast! I haven't had a thing to eat." But I just kept eating. I thought he'd pick it up and throw it away, but he didn't; so I just kept eating, and finished my breakfast.

Once in a while the Japs would have what they called a *yasume* day; it was like a day of rest, and they would give us beer and cakes. And as I said, we had money because the Japs had started paying us. We'd give some to one of the guards to go over and get some "caki" or some "beeru," and they'd run over and come back with it.

The beds for the six officers were lined up next to each other. We could lie down there at noon after lunch. You could take about half an hour for lunch. We'd finish eating, and then there would be about ten minutes when we could lie down, but the minute they went back to work, you had to sit up. Vandevelt and I would have liked to have gotten a good snooze in the afternoon, but we had to sit up. They put a guard around us.

The Filipinos had radios up in the mountains and they'd get direct broadcasts from the States. Every day they put out a little sheet and this sheet had all the latest news on the war straight from the United States. The Japs were trying to locate this radio station. They knew about it but they didn't know where the hell it was. Well, this middle-weight prize-fighter from Brooklyn used to get the sheets of news. He'd get them when he was out on work detail in Manila. Once when we had just lined up for roll call, I felt this thing in my hand—he had stuck a sheet in my hand. One of the Japs was watching. He knew something was going on. As soon as we broke up, I immediately went to the latrine and tore the stuff up and flushed it down the toilet. The Jap was right behind me and he came into the toilet, but it had already gone down. He searched me but found nothing.

I had a Rolls razor. When you sharpen those, they made a hell of a racket, and I used to sharpen it in the morning and then go down to the latrine area and shave. I was down there sharpening it and a Jap guard thought I was sending out a message. Then I showed him that it was just a razor and that I was shaving with it.

After I transferred to Camp #8, in the port area, we got much better news than we had in Bilibid (largely because of the information the prize-fighter gave me). So when I'd go back into Bilibid, which was about once a week, I used to tell all the news to a Colonel Johnson and Navy Commander Thomas Hayes. We used to sit down on the grass and I'd tell them all the news. I'd also give them information about what was going on in Manila; we could see how many ships were coming in and out of the harbor, that kind of thing. The Jap guard suspected what we were doing, so he'd come around and try to listen; when he did that, we'd switch the conversation immediately to something completely innocuous. Then as soon as he got out of hearing, we'd go back to the news.

For roll call we had to learn to count in Japanese.
You would learn rather rapidly; they lined us up, and
they'd say number one is *Ichi*. Then we go down the line
and say, *Ichi, Ichi, Ichi*. Two is *Ichi-Ni*. We'd go down the
line, *Ichi-Ni, Ichi-Ni*. And they'd go from one to the other,
and when they got to *Ichi-Ni-San*—*San* is three—some
began to miss it. When they did, they would get a whack
over the head with a baseball bat. So we quickly learned
to count in Japanese, although there was a colonel in
charge of us who never learned how to count. In fact, he
never learned a bit of Japanese, really. Strangely enough,
some of the so-called dumbest guys in the world with no
education would learn to speak Japanese and could talk
with the Japs, but some of the highly educated guys with
M.D.s, they never could communicate with them at all.
This one guy, the prize-fighter, he could talk Japanese
with them without any trouble.

Once, when they had caught a bunch of Filipinos
stealing some stuff downtown in Manila, they took them
over to Bataan and brought this guy, the prize-fighter,
along with them. Then they lined up the Filipinos and
cut their heads off one after another. They handed him
the sword and told him to be their guest and cut
somebody's head off. He said he couldn't do that. They
didn't force him to do it. But I think there were twenty-
five or twenty-six of them; they cut their heads off, one
after another, just because they caught them stealing.

I did occasionally think of escaping. I could have escaped a couple of times. I thought seriously of it, but if
you got caught they would just beat you. I saw two of
them that tried to escape, and all they pleaded for was
for the rest of us to kill them. They would tie them up
and every time one of the Japs would walk by, he'd hit
them with a stick. Oh, God! They'd be there with a broken jaw and nose smashed all over, in just terrible shape

and pleading, "For God's sake, shoot me! Get it over with!" Eventually they would kill them, but they would beat the hell out of them for two to three days first.

This happened to a close friend of mine, who had lived next to me before the war in the Philippines. When Wainwright surrendered, he didn't surrender. Instead he led a small guerrilla army of Filipinos up in the mountains. But one of the Filipinos told the Japs where he was, and they went and captured him. They brought him down to Bilibid. There was a section on the other side of the prison where they tied him up and beat the hell out of him every day for several days. They finally shot him. They buried him in the Chinese cemetery. I saw his wife after the war, but I couldn't tell her about that. I didn't want her to know how he died.

Of course, as doctors we had a certain status with the Japs. We never had to work at manual labor. After I moved to Camp #8, Captain Vandevelt and I had to hold sick call twice a day. First thing in the morning we'd holler, "Sick call!" There would be one or two new patients every day. We had a few drugs, some of the Red Cross stuff and some that the Japs had given us, and anybody that wanted to come on sick call, we would check them. We had thermometers, and if they had a fever and couldn't work we'd have to go to the Jap official and tell him the man was too sick to work. They'd usually let him stay in. But if you tried to get release time for somebody that they had just beaten up, that's when you got in trouble.

One time we were down in the port area on a work detail and one of the prisoners had offended the Japs in some way. As I say, if you got in trouble with them and then you were sick or got hurt or anything as a result, they wouldn't treat you. They had broken this guy's jaw and he was lying there. He couldn't swallow, couldn't chew or anything, the jaw was broken. I wanted to take him into Bilibid for treatment, and they wouldn't allow it. They let me take care of him but they kind of frowned on it. Ordinarily they wouldn't have taken care of him at all. But I couldn't do much.

Another time one of the men broke his arm and after a few days began to develop gangrene and a blood clot. The Japs were mad at him for some reason and wouldn't let me take him into the Bilibid hospital. Then this fellow developed pain in the stomach, and he started throwing up. So I told the Japs he had acute appendicitis, hoping thereby to get him in for treatment of the arm. So the Japs said, "If you're lying about this—we're going to go in with you and follow this—and if you're lying, you're going to have your head cut off." They didn't kid about these things, either. There was no sense of humor. It wasn't a joke. So we took him into Bilibid, and I went to the C.O. of the prison hospital, Commander Hayes— I knew him very well—and I said, "For God's sake, take this guy's appendix out, whether he needs it or not. It's not going to hurt him to have his appendix out, and if you don't, I'm going to get my head cut off." So they took him in and operated on him and took his appendix out, with this Jap standing there watching. Afterward the Jap came up to me and said, "He needed his appendix out." I don't know to this day if he had appendicitis or not.[4]

The two main kinds of sicknesses we had were dysentery—basilar or amoebic—and malaria. I had both of them. During the war over in Bataan one time I realized I was terribly thirsty. There were a lot of streams over there, beautiful-looking streams, but I knew that they weren't safe, so I had some canteen water instead. I got dysentery anyway, and I tell you I really had it. They took me into the hospital and they had to stop seven times on the way; I was passing blood. But when I got over to the hospital, Col. Frank Adamo started me on sulfadiazine (nobody had ever used it for dysentery), and it worked beautifully. It stopped my dysentery right in its tracks. I was in the hospital for about a week then.

In prison camp the Japs would give us bandages and three kinds of medicine. We asked them what they were for. They gave us rather general instructions: one was for here (pointing to the head); another one was for here (pointing to the heart); and the other was for here (pointing to the stomach). That's all the instructions we had. I didn't know what the hell they were. One was yellow and one was gray. The gray ones were pills, but the others were powders wrapped in rice paper.

Of course, quinine was a must. I always managed to save enough quinine to treat malaria, because I knew if you didn't have quinine and you had malaria, you were a dead duck. You wouldn't make it through, especially rundown the way we were. I got malaria on Bataan. I had a hell of a chill one night, the temp went up; it was just burning; I didn't have a thermometer, but it must have been about 105 degrees or so. I wanted to be sure that it was malaria, however, before I started treating it. With malaria usually you skip a night, and then you'll get your chill and fever again. But the next night I got it about the same time; about seven o'clock in the evening, I got the same chill and fever—I had a double dose of it. I had a hell of a dose. So I immediately started on the quinine. We took ten grains three times a day for four days, and then you'd take ten grains for about two months and that would wipe it out. I also had some Atabrine, which I took for about as long as I needed to, because it never recurred.

Manila was full of mosquitoes, and especially around the port area. Bilibid was about a mile from the port. The Red Cross sent some mosquito bars, and they were awfully good ones, a new type; the old type was made of

cotton and they kept out the air, so that they were awfully hot at night. You would just swelter in there. It could
be awfully hot in Manila. Before the war, for example,
Dode and I were once taking a walk downtown, and there
was a big thermometer. It read 96—this was about nine
or ten o'clock at night. It had cooled off; in the daytime
it would go over 100 every day, 101 or 102.

We had a surgical hospital in Bilibid. The Navy had
had a hospital there at Cavite, which is just outside Manila, before the war, and so after the surrender they just
moved the hospital and all the personnel from Cavite
straight into Bilibid. The Navy had quite a setup and
they did surgery. They could do major surgery, any kind
of surgery; they had some good surgeons.

During the war, before we were prisoners, we had a
nice supply of medical stuff; we had quite a supply of
morphine, codeine, a well-thought-out medical bag. But
after we became prisoners they confiscated it. We had
syringes—you would start a little fire there and sterilize
the needle. They had alcohol and you'd sterilize the needle
and mix up the morphine with water, and shoot it. During the war I did that quite a bit for my patients. I had a
stethoscope—they didn't take that—and a blood pressure cuff, some syringes, and a few other things. That
was it, all the medical equipment I had.

Sometimes the Jap enlisted men would come around,
asking us to treat them. They weren't supposed to. One
of them came around once, and I realized that he had
malaria. I took his temperature and it was 104. The Japs
had their headquarters up on the second floor of a building in the port area, and there was a long flight of stairs
going up there. I told him, "Go up and tell the sergeant
up there that you're sick, and that your temperature was
104 when I took it down here." So he went up there and

said that he had gone to me and I had taken his temperature and it was 104. The Jap that was in charge took him over to the stairs and told him to bend over. Then he got back and he gave him a hell of a kick. The guy rolled down those long stairs. That's what he got because he'd come to me.

On Corregidor, however, I know of one occasion at least when they let an American doctor treat a Jap soldier. That was Colonel Frank Adamo, who was a very fine surgeon, and a hell of a fine fellow too. One of the Japs had acute appendicitis and the Jap doctor was going to operate on him, but he let Adamo assist him. The Jap started out holding the scalpel the way you would hold a knife, and he made the incision as if he were stabbing somebody; he went down and he yanked at some organ but he couldn't find the appendix, so Adamo actually had to do the whole thing. Adamo reached in and pulled it out and tied it off—he took the appendix out and sewed the patient up. Colonel Adamo was very well liked by everybody. He was a very slick surgeon, very good.

When I was in Camp #8 we had this Jap in charge of us—we called him George, I don't know what the hell his real name was—but he kind of liked me. He used to take me into Manila with him on shopping tours. Sometimes we would stop and get some so-called ice cream. One time on one of those outings, the Filipinos kept trying to shove stuff in my pockets. We rode on a streetcar, and they kept handing me money and other things surreptitiously. But I kept pushing it back. I didn't want it. George knew that something was going on, but he didn't know what. It's lucky I didn't take anything, because just before we got back to camp, he went over every stitch, every pocket I had, and, of course, I had nothing. If I'd have had anything, he'd have raised hell about it.

At the entrance to the prison there was a hospital office building run by the Americans. One time this George said to one of the Americans there, "Why don't you cure some of these people here in this hospital?" The guy replied, "Well, if you gave us any decent food, they would recover." So George takes his sword out and goes after him in a rage. He just took his saber out and went after him, and got this guy in a corner. The guy held up a chair before him and the Jap was hammering at him. He'd have killed him if he could have gotten any closer. Finally I walked up and said, "George, it's time for us to go." So he put his sword back and he came with me. Everybody in Bilibid heard this story, and they treated me as though I had a pet lion going around with me, because they would disappear when I would show up with this guy in tow.

We always had nicknames for the guards. We'd call them "George" or "Baggy Pants" or something. There was a little ceremony they'd have every night. They'd face Japan, face the emperor, and they'd sing a song and then they'd bow to him. And on his birthday they each got a little piece of cake, a little two-square-inch piece of birthday cake for the emperor. George had me in his office on the emperor's birthday once, and he said, "Roosevelt, no good!" He turned to me and said, "Know that—Roosevelt—no good!" I said, "Roosevelt is my commander; your commander is Tojo." I said, "I can't say anything against my commander." He understood that.

There was a time that I got slapped by a guard. We had an awful dumb person who had athlete's foot and this Jap guard had some cotton swabs and was dipping them into hydrochloric acid and putting it on the guy's feet. I told him to stop it. He took me in another room and he whacked me one, but he didn't go back and put more hydrochloric acid on the foot. He'd have burned the hell out of it if he did.

We had a lot of medicine in Bilibid sent over by the Red Cross, but it was awfully hard to get it out of the Japs. I guess they thought the war was going to last about a hundred years the way they acted. You put a requisition in for drugs and they would cut it by about 90 percent. If you asked for one hundred of something, they would give you ten. So first I asked for some vitamins; I asked for a hundred vitamins and I ended up with ten— ten tablets, which wasn't going to help a hundred and fifty men very much. So then I asked for several thousand and I got about a thousand, and instead of tablets I asked for bottles. Finally, I got at least a hundred and fifty bottles of vitamins, and I gave one to each of the men.

Also, they would give you only some of the equipment you needed, which often made the part you did have ineffective. For instance, if you're going to use ether on a person, you've got to have a mask, of course. Well, the Japs might give you the ether, but they wouldn't give you the mask, or they'd give you the mask but no ether. None of it made any sense. They had a theory that if you walked into a building, you had to step in some material right at the entrance with your shoes on before you came into the building, and that was supposed to keep you from bringing any bugs into the building. Pure superstition!

At one point the Japs began pulling these Filipinos off the streets and putting them in Jap uniforms. The way they "recruited" them was they'd send a truck around and any of these guys they could catch was in for the duration. They'd put a uniform on him. They had one of these guys guarding us, and every time he went by us, he'd stop and start singing, "We're in the Marianas; We're in the Marianas; We're in the Marianas and it won't be long now." He would keep singing that for about an hour. He was telling us that the U.S. fleet was coming across the Pacific, and the Marianas were getting pretty close to Japan.

One night in Bilibid we had to report to the hospital on the other side of the parade ground. It was pitch dark; remember, we all had night blindness—we couldn't see a thing. To get there we had to pass a little stream about six feet below the level of the ground. I was leading, and I said to Captain Poweleit, one of the other doctors, "I can't see a damn thing!" Poweleit said, "I think I can see." So I said, "Well, you go ahead and take the lead then." So Poweleit went ahead and the first thing I knew he had stepped off a ledge—he couldn't see anything either— and landed head first way down in the ditch. Finally, he pulled himself out, and then we tried crawling our way over to the hospital. Then a Jap guard heard us. We were crawling around on our hands and knees, and he started hollering and yelling. I was afraid he would start shooting, so I said to Poweleit, "We've got to make some noise here." We started singing, and when he heard that then he was all right. He knew we weren't trying anything. Finally we got over to the hospital where we had to line up.

After we'd been prisoners for a while, the Japs for propaganda purposes let us send messages back to our families. They sent them out by radio from Tokyo. Major Breslin heard about it and said, "Come on, we can send a message back to our families!" So we ran after this Jap general who was in charge of it and caught up with him and asked if he'd send a message for us. He said, "So you want to send a message?"

We both said, "Yeah, hell, yes!"

"Well," he said, "what are you going to say?"

Breslin said to me under his breath, "Tell them the steaks are a little tough." Fortunately, this general didn't understand much English. He asked me, "What are you going to say?"

There were two choices; you could say you were being treated "good," or you were being treated "fair." If you said you were being treated "good," they'd send the message off; if you said you were being treated "fair," that was it. It wouldn't go. Well, I wanted the message to go back to my family, so they'd know I was still alive. Dode hadn't heard from me since before the fall of Corregidor. She went a good year without hearing a thing. She didn't know if I was dead or alive. So I said, "Good." And they sent that back. I think I might have gotten some criticism for that, but I never heard about it after the war.

Later, while I was still in Bilibid, in the fall of 1942, they were sending a detail south down to the southern islands, to Mindanao, and Breslin and I decided we would go. You could volunteer for it. But when they called out all the names, we weren't called, and I said, "Breslin, what the hell, I thought we were on that list to go." "Oh," he said, "I changed it. I told them we didn't want to go." As it turned out, it's lucky we didn't go, because they had a hell of a time down there. They were down there for months, and when they came back they were wrecks. The trips on the Jap ships were about the worst thing that you can imagine. And they had been right on the equator—hot as the devil. They also said the food was bad; it was just a very poor detail.

Then one day [September 21, 1944]—I think it was the prettiest sight I ever saw—we were standing in the middle of the prison yard in Bilibid and I looked up and first I saw one plane. Then five minutes later the sky was covered with them. The Japs said they were practice planes, but all of a sudden they began to peel off and commence precision bombing. They were U.S. Navy planes. They bombed the harbor and kept it up for about four days. Later, when we were leaving on the prison ship, I could see they'd hit nearly every ship in the harbor— and it's a big harbor. They also dropped leaflets that had MacArthur's "I shall return" on them. I got one of those leaflets.

That's what life was like the first couple of years in prison camp."

Notes

1. See Charles C. Roland, "Allied POWs, Japanese Captors and the Geneva Convention," *War & Society* 9, no. 2 (October 1991): 83–101.

2. Willard H. Waterous, "Reminiscences of Dr. W. H. Waterous Pertinent to World War II in the Philippines," unpublished manuscript, 1953, Center of Military History, Washington, DC, 114. For Hayes's role in the intelligence-gathering network see Thomas Hayes, *Bilibid Diary: The Secret Notebooks of Commander Thomas Hayes, POW, the Philippines, 1942–45*, ed. A. B. Feuer (Hamden, CT: Archon, 1987). See also the letter from Franz Weissblatt, March 13, 1945, to Josephine Devigne Donovan (cited in Chapter 8), which also indicates that Captain Donovan was part of an informal intelligence-gathering operation.

3. Julien M. Goodman, M.D., *M.D.P.O.W.* (New York: Exposition Press, 1972), 103. Goodman mentions encountering Captain Donovan on one further occasion, at the end of August 1944, at which time he and Vandevelt "stressed the belief that the Allied return to the Philippines was imminent" (107).

4. Captain Donovan kept a list of the patients, their diagnoses, and treatment in Camp #8 (a list he still has). It records that on "April 6" (1943) a "Stacy, James C." had a "Fractured left ulnea— splint applied to arm pain. . . . Permission was given to stay in bed. While in bed patient developed pain in abdomen, with vomiting. The pain localized in the right lower abdomen. Sent to hosp. April 15th." Also, "Irwin, Willard H. April 7. Fr. mandible. 1. Bandage applied to jaw . . . examination revealed swelling and crepitation at angle of jaw right side."

These incidents were also recounted in two depositions submitted for the war crimes trials after the war. The first, by T/Sgt. Martin E. Quirk, recorded on May 17, 1945, notes:

"In May 1943, a young American soldier whose name I do not now remember, but who was a prisoner of war sent from Bilibid Prison Hospital on a work detail at the Motor Pool and Repair Shop, was doing some work on the rear axle assembly of a Jap truck. The assembly was on a jack and detached from the truck itself, which was suspended by a crane. The axle assembly slipped off the jack and fell on the left arm of the American prisoner. The boy lay there rolling back and forth in pain and four of us started toward him to carry him to the barracks for treatment but a Japanese private named Fakuda (phonetic spelling) who was in charge of the section in which we were working at the time refused to let us go near him for nearly an hour. Finally we were permitted to carry the boy to our barracks where Capt. William Donovan, MC . . . attempted to set the arm. We had no adequate medication or equipment there and I cut some emergency splints for temporary use. The injured prisoner had a compound comminuted fracture of both bones in the left forearm which required a traction splint, and the appearance of the arm indicated clearly that there was a bad internal hemorrhage. The Jap supervisor, Fakuda, went to the barracks with us when we carried the injured boy over there and all during the time that Captain Donovan was trying to set the arm, the Jap stood there cursing the boy and kicking him. When the American began to cry from the pain and shock, the Jap gave him a hard back-hand slap in the face.

"Captain Donovan knew that there was great danger of gangrene in the arm from the extreme hematoma and internal blood clot, which would result in the loss of the arm or perhaps the life of the injured prisoner, and he tried to get the Japanese in charge to let the American be taken to the Bilibid Prison Hospital where they were equipped to treat him properly. But this was denied. After the injured prisoner had lain in the barracks for three or four days, he developed an acute attack of appendicitis, with a temperature of 104°. Capt. Donovan made repeated trips to the next room in the barracks building to attempt to persuade the Japanese to permit the sick American to be taken to the hospital for an operation. Finally, after about a half day of this, a Jap medical corpsman was sent to look at the sick prisoner, after which authority was given to take the American prisoner to the hospital. If it had not been for the appendicitis the soldier would probably have died.

"On one of the trips to attempt to persuade the Japanese to let the American be taken to the hospital, Captain Donovan was slapped, he told us (and I could hear the slap in the next room)."

(Item #40-1003, Record Group 153, National Archives, College
Park, MD.)

The second deposition is by T/Sgt. Volnie S. Burk, taken
April 24, 1945. Excerpts follow:

Q. What were the circumstances surrounding the beating of
Corporal Erwin?

A. This occurred at Port Area during the month of May 1943,
I do not remember the exact date. We were doing extra duty moving junk and spare parts in a building at our camp. We were doing
this extra duty because the Japs had accused us of insulting one of
their officers. We were . . . under the supervision of a Jap guard
who was a corporal in the Japanese Army, his name was Hiashia.
. . . The first thing I knew the guard was beating Corporal Erwin
with his fists. Erwin did not fight back but just warded off the
blows, which made the guard furious. The guard struck at Corporal Erwin with a piece of iron and missed and from then on used
his fists. . . . Just before they dismissed us for the night they lined
us up and the same guard beat Corporal Erwin again. . . .

Q. Did Corporal Erwin sustain any injuries in or as a result of
the beating?

A. Yes sir, his jaw was broken in three places and he was badly
bruised as a result of the beating given him.

Q. Was Corporal Erwin given any medical treatment for his
injuries?

A. The Japs did not give him any treatment for this injury unless he agreed to sign a statement saying he fell down the steps.
Corporal Erwin refused to sign such a statement.

Q. Did any medical officer see Corporal Erwin?

A. Yes sir, Capt. W. Donovan and Capt. W. Vandervilt[*sic*]
. . . saw Corporal Erwin and I believe Captain Donovan set his jaw
for him.

Q. Did either of the two captains sign any statement showing
Corporal Erwin had fallen down the steps?

A. No sir, they were asked to sign such a statement and refused
to do so. (Item #40-187, Record Group 153, National Archives,
College Park, MD.)

5

The Prison Ship "Horror *Maru*"

BY THE SUMMER OF 1944 the tide of the war was running in the Allies' favor. Significant victories near the Palau Islands in early 1944 placed the Allied forces only six hundred to seven hundred miles from the southernmost island in the Philippines, Mindanao. Thus began MacArthur's famous "leap-frogging" tactics to regain the Philippines and proceed to Japan. As noted, on September 21, 1944, American bombers began daily attacks on Manila and the port area; a number of Japanese ships were sunk in Manila harbor. MacArthur's celebrated return to the Philippines occurred on October 20, with the invasion of Leyte, an island about midpoint in the Philippine island chain. On wading ashore that day, MacArthur made this announcement: "People of the Philippines, I have returned! By the grace of Almighty God, our forces stand again on Philippine soil."[1]

On January 9, 1945, the Allied forces landed on Luzon at Lingayen Gulf, where three years earlier the Japanese had invaded. On February 4, Bilibid Prison was recaptured, and on March 3, Manila was again under Allied control. The city, however, had been reduced to rubble and the Filipino populace subjected to a massive campaign of savage atrocities by the departing Japanese.

Most of the American prisoners of war who were still in passable health had been shipped up north to Japan, Formosa, and other points. Only those too weak to travel remained in camps like Bilibid. MacArthur visited Bilibid shortly after its liberation. He later observed, "I will never know how the 800 prisoners there survived for three long years. . . . The men who greeted me were scarcely more than skeletons. . . . They remained silent. . . . I looked down the lines of men bearded and soiled . . . with ripped and soiled shirts and trousers . . . with suffering and torture written on their gaunt faces. Here," he continued, "was all that was left of my men of Bataan and Corregidor."[2]

Many thousands of POWs had met an even worse fate, however—hellish voyages on Japanese prison ships. Shipment of prisoners north began in earnest as the Allied forces made their advances. A group of 1,035 prisoners left Manila on August 25, 1944, aboard the *Noto Maru*. Several other ships left in September; many of these were sunk by Allied bombs or torpedoes. Contrary to the Geneva Convention, the Japanese did not mark prison ships. One historian has noted, "The single worst time for a POW to be on the water was September 1944."[3]

American POWs from Bilibid Prison in Manila about to embark on one of the "hell ships" bound for Japan, Fall 1944. *National Archives*

The ship that Captain Donovan was on officially left Manila on October 1, 1944 (it did not actually leave the harbor, however, until October 3). It was the *Harō Maru*, which the POWs dubbed the "Horror *Maru*," considered to be one of the worst—if not the worst—of them all. It arrived in Takao Harbor, Formosa, on October 24 or 25, with a ten-day layover (from October 11 to 21) in the port of Hong Kong. While in Hong Kong the boat's convoy was strafed on at least one occasion (October 15 or 16) by American planes of the 14th U.S. Air Force based in China. On November 5 or 6 the ship left Takao briefly but returned later in the day. The prisoners were not allowed to debark in Takao until November 8. Thus, they spent a total of thirty-nine days aboard the *Harō Maru*.[4]

On October 11 the *Arisan Maru* left Manila. This vessel, the so-called "October ship," was sunk thirteen days later with a loss of 1,802 prisoners; only eight survived. One of them, Sgt. Avery Wilbur, of Appleton, Wisconsin, was contacted in February 1945 by Mrs. Donovan, who was seeking information about her husband, upon Wilbur's return to the States (see Chapter 8). Four other survivors were picked up by a Japanese destroyer and eventually placed on the *Harō Maru* while it was docked in Formosa.

The "December ship," the *Oryoku Maru*—the last prison ship to leave before the Philippines was recaptured—departed on December 13, 1944. Its fate was not much better than that of the "October ship." It was sunk shortly after leaving Manila with a loss of several hundred. Those who survived were put on two other ships, one of which, the *Enoura Maru*, was bombed in Takao harbor in Formosa. Of the 1,619 prisoners (two-thirds of whom were officers) who had boarded the *Oryoku Maru* in Manila, fewer than 400 survived. In all, twenty-

five prison ships were bombed or torpedoed. An estimated
11,000 POWs died at sea, out of 50,000 shipped.[5] Nearly
5,000—or three out of four—died at sea during the fall
of 1944.[6]

The *Harō Maru*, Captain Donovan's ship, was a
6,000- to 8,000-ton antiquated wooden freighter about
the size of a Mississippi riverboat.[7] It had two holds: one
had been for horses, its floor still had horse manure; the
other was lined with coal. Captain Donovan started the
trip in the latter, sharing the space with seven hundred
to eight hundred others, crammed into a fifty-four-
hundred-square-foot area. This meant that each person
had a space about two-and-one-half-feet square.

Along with American POWs were one hundred to
two hundred British and Dutch prisoners, the only survivors of another prison ship that had been sunk off
Manila Bay, the *Toyofuku Maru*; it had evacuated prisoners from the Dutch East Indies in February 1944. Altogether, eleven hundred POWs were crammed into the
holds of the *Harō Maru*.

The conditions on all the prison ships were unspeakable, certainly among the most heinous treatment any
prisoners or concentration camp inmates received during the war. The temperature in the hold in the first
couple of days while the ship lay at anchor in Manila
probably reached 120 degrees. At first there were no water rations; prisoners had to live on what they had in
their canteens. Food consisted of one large ball of rice—
or approximately a pint—a day. There were no sanitary
facilities. Latrine buckets were lowered into the hold and
circulated. Often these would slop over and collapse as
they were raised up to the deck.

Because of the lack of water many died of dehydration. Water canteens were a prized object, and many were
stolen. Many men went crazy—some from having drunk

urine or sea water in their desperation. Several of those who went insane were killed by other prisoners. One prison ship survivor later commented: "It was sheer madness. A page out of Dante's *Inferno* couldn't describe the spectacle of humans sunk to the level of animals . . . sickness, humiliations, living . . . in a . . . dark, rancid-smelling hold with filth, human excrement, sweating, dirty bodies ready to scream in despair and anguish."[8] In 1947, Major Donovan's testimony about the prison ship was submitted as a deposition for the war crimes trials (see Appendix). It is now in the National Archives.

"As the Americans returned to the Philippines in the fall of 1944, the Japs began transporting prisoners up north, to Japan, Formosa, and China. I was sent out on the *Harō Maru*—all the Jap ships were called *Maru*. We called it the "Horror *Maru*." The trip on that ship— thirty-nine hellish days—was indescribable, the worst part of the whole war for me.

There were several ships. Many were sunk, with hundreds of lives lost. I had volunteered for a ship that went down; it had lots of doctors on it—twenty-six, I think— and several of my friends. It left in October and was sunk by an American torpedo. They didn't mark the ships as prison ships. Eighteen hundred men were lost. It was torpedoed three days out of port. This was known as the "October ship." Mine was the "September ship." There was also a "December ship" that was hit with a lot of losses. I'd volunteered for the October ship. I asked Nogi, the camp commandant at Bilibid, if I could get on that ship. He said he'd look into it, but he came back after a couple of days and said it was too much trouble to change the list, so I was put on the other one. This was just another example of how much is a matter of chance. In all of these experiences it seems that a lot of people were killed just by chance—one person would be killed if he were a couple of feet ahead of you, or if he got on the wrong ship.

So when the time came to leave, they marched us through the port area and loaded us on the ship, and put us down in the hold. We sat there in the harbor for a couple of days before we started. Sweltering! It was at least 120 degrees down in the hold where we were staying. It was hot—oh, God, it was hot! We were on the ship thirty-nine days and we had thirty-six deaths, most of them occurring the first ten days. We were supposedly heading for Japan but we ended up in Formosa.

The ship was a wooden freighter. It was about six or eight thousand tons. There were two holds and on the floor of our hold was coal. The ship held about twelve hundred men altogether, prisoners and Japs. Our hold held about seven to eight hundred, the smaller one about four hundred. The hold was about twenty yards wide. The larger hold was about twenty by twenty-five yards, and the smaller one was about ten by twenty yards. There were eight hundred men in an area of about six hundred square yards in 120-degree heat.

The nearest person was right on top of you. We were just piled in there. The first night I had about two guys with their legs piled on top of me. The next day they called for volunteers; they needed a couple of doctors back in the other hold. I volunteered immediately. I thought, "Jesus, it can't be any worse than this." So I said to Poweleit, "Al, come on, we'll volunteer and go back there." So we did and it was better.

When we were down in the hold they had two guys up on deck who had a pail that you were supposed to leak in. They'd pass it around and finally they'd pull it up and empty it and send it back down again. They had an old rope that was worn out when they started using it and it would break and spill the pail, spraying us all over with urine. Once there was a chaplain sitting next to me; he came over because he thought there was a little more room. The place was crowded, about a third of the men couldn't find a place to sit. They would hang around up against the walls. So I passed this bucket full of urine over to him, and apparently I was hanging on to the top of it, so about a quart or so of it fell on his head. He roared, "God Almighty, Doctor!" I said, "I can't see what the hell I'm doing here." He got up and moved.

For food, they'd give us a rice ball about the size of a large softball. Each one would get a ball of rice, and that was to last all day. Usually they'd issue that very early in the morning, about 4 or 5 A.M., and it was usually gone by about 7 or 8 o'clock. That was the last you got until the next morning. There wasn't room enough to sit down for all the prisoners, so, as I say, about a third of them just sort of bounced around. As a prisoner you usually had a little group that you were in—groups of three or four—and when one of the other prisoners would come into your area, you'd throw him out. You'd just push him away. And some of them were just sort of thrown around; they never did have a place to sit down. Some of them fixed up a little hammock on the side of the wall, and then they stayed up there.

In that ship there was a British officer who had come from the River Kwai, over in Thailand. The Japs had brought him back to Singapore and put him on a ship in February, and he was down in the hold of this ship till June or July, when he finally got to Manila. The ship he was on was bombed and he drifted around Manila Bay for a couple of days before, finally, the Japs picked him up and dropped him off in Bilibid. He had been working on that bridge on the River Kwai back in Thailand.

There was also a guy on his ship who had acute appendicitis, and they took the guy's appendix out in the hold of the ship—quite a story.

Anyway, this British officer's name was Lewis. Actually he was a Welshman. He also was a magician. He could do card tricks. He went with us up to Formosa, and then Poweleit and I and this guy bunked together. He was quite a card shark. He could do a lot of card tricks. He said he was a member of the magicians' league. On Formosa he showed us how to do some of his tricks but not others. They were worth money to him. He would say, "This trick cost me five bucks." He used to buy them.

For a while on the ship they didn't give us any water. You just had whatever was in your canteen. If we made any noise, if the men began hollering, the Japs would start firing indiscriminately. Some of the men went crazy, and some of them were just murdered. There were about seven of them, and when they'd go crazy they'd start yelling, and then the Japs would start shooting. See, they'd start yelling and hollering and the Japs didn't want any noise, and so they'd say, "Shut up or we're going to start shooting." And they'd just shoot indiscriminately at anybody. So when one of these guys would go crazy and started hollering, we had to shut him up. The other prisoners would kill him. They'd hit him with their canteens—their canteens were full of water. They'd bang on his head. When you hit a person with that, it's a real blow. They beat them to death. They killed about seven of them that way. Then they'd just take them and throw them over the side.

They had two prisoners on the upper deck, and every morning they would holler down, "Look around and see if there's any dead lying around." If there were, they would tie a rope to them, haul them up, take off all their clothes, and over the side they would go. That was the

burial. Every morning you'd look around and see if anyone had died near you, and, if so, they'd tie a rope around
him and pull him up and throw him over.

One time I went up on deck to ask the Japs to give us
more water. And I left my water canteen behind with
Poweleit. I said to him, "Keep an eye on my canteen.
Don't let anybody take it." When I came back the canteen was gone. I said to Poweleit, "Where the hell is my
canteen?" He looked around. Somebody had taken it. So
he addressed the others; he said, "Why, here this doctor
has just gone up on deck, taken a personal risk, to try to
get more water for us and while he's gone you steal his
canteen." He told them that was worthless behavior. Well,
suddenly the canteen reappeared. They handed it forward. I guess he shamed them into giving it back.

There was nothing to do. We just sat there all day
with these buckets going around full of urine and everything. We didn't shave. There was hardly enough air to
breathe. I wore the same uniform, the same clothes, the
entire trip. I did have shoes. A lot of them didn't have
shoes. No showers. It wasn't exactly a luxury cruise.

We had a number of deaths down there, and they
had to have a doctor to sign the death certificates. One
time I started to go up on deck for that when this guy by
the name of Farris, who was an awful ass if there ever was
one, told them they didn't need me, that he could sign
the certificates. "Stay down," they said, "we don't need
you, we have doctor so and so." I said, "He's not a doctor. He's a dentist. He can't sign death certificates." So I
went up to the headquarters of the ship. In the front hold
there was a lieutenant colonel, medical officer, and I was
a captain. They had the two of us there to sign the death
certificates. They turned to this lieutenant colonel and
asked him, "What did this guy die of?"

"Well," he said, "lack of air and lack of water."

They said, "Jesus, you can't say that. We've got to send this in to Tokyo."

So the Jap turned to me and said, "What did this guy die of?"

"He died of anoxia and dehydration," I said. It means the same thing, of course.

"What's that, what's that mean?" he asked me.

I said, "It's . . ." and I pointed vaguely toward my heart. He didn't know what the hell I was talking about. That's what they sent in to Tokyo. Anything to do with prisoners of war went straight to Tokyo. I knew they had about half a dozen Japs, probably born in the United States, who knew English, and as soon as they got that message, they would understand what I was talking about. So the crew immediately got orders to give us all the water we wanted and also to let the prisoners up on deck. From then on we got all the water we needed. And also from then on they said that as long as the military situation allowed it, we could be on deck. So about nine-tenths of the time we were. We set up a kind of rotation system where about a third rotated up on deck at a time. Once they started that, it relieved things in the hold.

I was sort of running the rotation operation for the officers. They'd tell me I could put so many up on deck. I think there were twenty officers I could put up. So I'd call them by name. I knew them all, so I'd call out the names. Then they'd lie on the deck—there was an area on the deck that was covered with canvas tarpaulins that had room for about twenty.

Most of the men were too weak to get up on deck, though. To get up you had to climb a ladder that angled backward at the top. You had to damn near chin yourself to get up. It was a tough job to get out of there. Most of them were too weak to think of going up. There was a doctor on the ship, an orthopedic surgeon, who died.

He was sick when we started and we didn't want him to come. He didn't have to come, but he wanted to. He died after about two or three days.

It was a very dangerous time. When you were out at sea, you were fairly safe; the American submarines would stay around the ports. But if you got near a port like Hong Kong or Manila, that's when it was dangerous. One night we heard a tapping on the side of the ship. This Navy guy said radar had hit us. Some of the prisoners were Navy men, and they said they could hear the radar hitting the side of the ship. After the war, after we were repatriated, I asked some submarine men if it was possible to hear it, and they said, yes, you could. You could hear the radar hitting the side of the ship. One time when I was up on deck I saw a torpedo just miss the ship by a few feet. Another time I saw three Japanese ships going down at one time—all hit by American torpedoes. One Navy guy told me there were so many ships out there, they would just fire at random. Altogether four ships in our convoy were torpedoed.

Years later Dode said that even though she didn't know where I was, during those ten days I was on the ship she was the most worried. Avery Wilbur, who was from Wisconsin, was one of the five who managed to get ashore in China when his ship was sunk. They got into a little boat and got to shore, and the Chinese took him all the way across China and finally back to the United States. It got a lot of publicity, but the War Department told him to shut up and not to discuss it. So he was afraid to talk. Dode called him and talked to him, but she didn't get much information out of him, except he said that he knew me. And he was almost positive that I was not on the ship that went down, the ship that he was on, the October ship. That was the one that went down with eighteen hundred, twenty-six of them doctors. Dode and

my folks knew about the ships going down and they knew
I had been shipped on one of the ships, but they didn't
know which one. So they were trying to find out, and
that's why Dode called.

Then there was a Colonel Craig, who had been a good
friend of mine before the surrender, and he kept track of
me and also kept track of my things. When I left the
Philippines on that ship, he stayed there in Bilibid. So I
gave him a big footlocker full of stuff that I couldn't take
with me. He kept it and after the war had it shipped
back home to Madison, where I got it back. Also, when
Bilibid was liberated he and some of the others contacted
Dode about me. They had heard that I made it up to
Japan. But that wasn't until March in 1945.

After leaving Manila on the "Horror *Maru*," we were
at sea for about ten days, and finally we began to pass
some islands. We didn't know where the hell we were,
because when you took off in one of those ships you never
knew where the hell you were going. So after about ten
days, one of the British officers was up on deck; and he
looked up and suddenly said, "By George! It's Hong
Kong!" He had been stationed in Hong Kong before the
war and recognized it. We were surprised. We had arrived in the harbor of Hong Kong, a beautiful harbor!
We sat there for a couple of weeks, and then the American bombers began coming over from the Philippines.
Some of these were big ones, flying awfully high, and
they'd bomb the port area of Hong Kong. They'd come
over every day about the same time. They were flying so
high that the Jap planes couldn't reach them. Once in a
while a smaller plane would come over, apparently from
China. They'd come over and fly low and strafe our ship,
and when that happened the Japs would pull off in a
small boat and sit out in the harbor and leave the ship.

We'd be sitting down there in the hold without any guards.

So we crossed the China Sea and stopped in Hong Kong for two weeks. That was the most pleasant time of all; the weather was perfect—sleeping out on the top deck. While we were in Hong Kong, the Japs said we could send somebody ashore and buy some mess and food. I borrowed twenty bucks from a guy next to me and gave it to this Farris, the dentist, who was going to go ashore. He bought a duck and cooked it, but he ate most of it himself. For my twenty bucks I got a piece of meat that you could put on a teaspoon. I had two enlisted corpsmen that worked for me on the ship, and I borrowed ten bucks from each of them. When we got back to San Francisco, one of them appeared and started with a long story about his wife being sick. I said, "What do you want, that ten dollars back?" He said, "Yeah." I had about a hundred dollars on me that night. I gave him back his ten. He disappeared. That's the last I ever saw of him.

I could have escaped in the Hong Kong harbor. The ship was anchored up a river not far from shore, and I could have gotten off. We had a little shack on the deck there, and it held all the medical supplies. It had a sort of open window, no glass in it, just an opening. I could have gone through that and I could have gotten down to the water without the Japs seeing me and then swum to shore. I'd have taken my shoes off and tied them around my neck, but I figured it was too big of a risk. They'd have nailed me if they'd seen me.

They wanted to get us up to Japan, so they put us on this ship and we sailed off again, up between Taiwan and China. We were getting up toward Japan, but the U.S. fleet had broken through, and they were bombing the coast of China heavily. So our ship suddenly stopped, turned around, and went back. They dropped us off in Takao, Taiwan.

After we landed in Takao, they marched us through the town. The natives gathered along the streets and spit at us and threw stones and garbage at us. Then they loaded us on a train and took us to a camp in southern Formosa near a place called Kagi, and we stayed there in a relatively nice camp for the rest of the war. "

Notes

1. As cited in Spector, *Eagle against the Sun*, 428.
2. MacArthur, *Reminiscences*, 248.
3. Daws, *Prisoners of the Japanese*, 286.
4. The main sources for the ship's chronology are William R. Evans, *Kora!* (Rogue River, OR: Atwood, 1986), 118–20, and Goodman, *M.D.P.O.W.*, 114–26, both of whom kept diaries or logbooks aboard ship.

Forrest Knox in Daws's *Prisoners of the Japanese* generally corroborates the Evans and Goodman dates (292). See also Dorothy Cave, *Beyond Courage: One Regiment against Japan, 1941–1945*, rev. ed. (Las Cruces, NM: Yucca Tree, 1996), 294–97.

5. Daws, *Prisoners of the Japanese*, 297.
6. Spector, *Eagle against the Sun*, 400; Evans, *Kora!*, 109–10.
7. Alvin C. Poweleit, *USAFFE* (privately printed, 1975), 121. I follow the consensus of most historians that this was the name of the ship and use it throughout. In his postwar deposition for the war crimes trials, however, Major Donovan referred to the ship as the *Dai-Nitchi Maru*. This name appears to have been an error, since the ship and voyage are clearly the same as that labeled the *Harō Maru* by others. The fact that the prisoners called it the "horror maru" suggests either that they were adapting "harō" to "horror," or that historians have mistakenly called it the *Harō Maru* after the POWs' ironic epithet. In a letter addressed to the editor, dated September 5, 1997, Capt. Teruaki Kawano, of the Military History Department at the National Institute for Defense Studies in Tokyo, writes that there is no record of a *Harō Maru* in its shipping list files.

8. Adrian R. Martin, *Brothers from Bataan: POWs, 1942–1945* (Manhattan, KS: Sunflower, 1992), 191.

6

Formosa

THERE WERE SEVERAL POW camps on Formosa, now called Taiwan. Captain Donovan, along with the other doctors and their patients from the ship, was interned in Camp #6, a medical camp, at Shirakawa near the city of Kagi from November 1944 until the liberation in late August 1945. Conditions were somewhat better on Formosa than in the Philippines, but the years of near starvation, malnutrition, and stress had seriously weakened even those who had escaped more serious beatings and injury. In addition, there were occasional strafings and bombings by American planes, because the camp was not marked.[1] However, morale was much higher than it had been earlier in the war, because the prisoners knew the tide had turned and that their hour of liberation lay in the not too distant future.

Shortly after the recapture of the Philippines the Allied forces won other strategic victories—at Iwo Jima in March 1945 and on Okinawa in June. Okinawa was about three hundred miles to the northeast of Formosa, or about an hour's flight from the southern coast of Japan. High-level bombing continued against Japan. A devastating firebombing raid over Tokyo by B-29s on March 9–10—the biggest air raid in history to that date—destroyed much of the city, killing eighty thousand persons. Meanwhile, V-E Day in Europe occurred May 8, 1945. Finally, after the Nagasaki bombing on August 9, the

Japanese surrendered unconditionally on August 15 (August 14, U.S. time).

It is now known that Japanese policy in the waning days of the war was to kill all POWs. Captured Japanese instructions issued at the prison camp of Taihoku in Formosa ordered that prisoners were to be "disposed of" and "annihilated": "Whether they are destroyed individually or in groups . . . with mass bombings, poisonous smoke, poisons, drowning, decapitation, or what, dispose of the prisoners as the situation dictates. In any case it is the aim not to allow the escape of a single one, to annihilate them all, and not to leave any traces."[2] But although isolated incidents of POW massacres had occurred earlier—the most notable at Palawan in the Philippines, for example, where 138 were executed on December 14, 1944—after the unconditional surrender in mid-August, such orders were not carried out.

At the time of the surrender Captain Donovan weighed about 120 pounds (down from a norm of about 150–155). Shortly after the surrender American planes began dropping food and supplies, and on August 29, Allied forces landed on the island. By early September approximately 14,950 American POWs in the Far East had been liberated. More than one in three of their comrades, however—or about 10,650 men—had died in the camps.[3]

"I was on Formosa about nine months in what had been a Japanese camp by the name of Shirakawa. It consisted of several buildings, more like shacks really. The number of prisoners there varied a lot, because they'd leave them there a while and then ship them up north. They wanted to use the prisoners as bargaining chips.

We had a hospital with two wards. The commanding medical officer, Lt. Col. Harold Glattly, assigned one ward

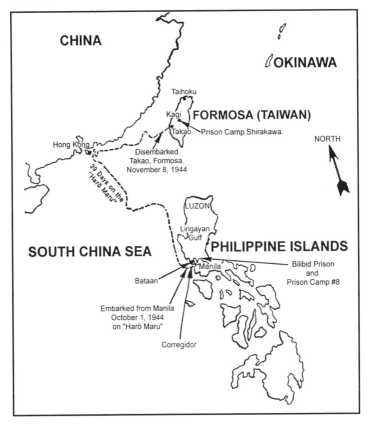

to me and one ward to Captain Poweleit. We had nine or ten doctors there, but they had nothing to do. So we used to rotate on two-hour shifts every day: 9 to 11; 11 to 1; 1 to 3; 3 to 5; and 5 to 7. I got to know Glattly there. I had known him from the Philippines, so when I got there, he said, "Bill, pick out someone that you want to help you, and the two of you will work there." I picked Poweleit.

We had a fire they kept going most of the time with a big bowl of boiling water. We could get water, not fresh water, but sterile water. We'd keep our canteens full of sterile water. There was a stream running near the camp where we washed our mess gear, but it was full of rats running all over the place. After we'd wash our mess gear we'd go and dip it in the boiling water, and none of us ever got typhoid fever. But the British idea of sanitation was about zero. They had the idea that if it looked clean, it was clean. They never boiled their water; they'd clean their mess gear in this little stream with all these rats, and then they'd rub the inside of it with sand and get it shining, wash it out again, and then hang it up. Then they'd eat out of that. Every one of them came down with typhoid fever, and only one American, who was living with them, came down with typhoid. So I had a ward full of typhoid fever, and the other ward was full of TB cases, pulmonary TB. We had no X-rays, of course, for diagnosis. We had the stethoscope, but these cases were so far advanced that it was easy to diagnose them. We did have some antityphoid vaccine, but only 1 cc. of it. Glattly wanted to give it to the doctors who would be treating the patients, but he wasn't sure how to distribute it. I said you need only 1/10 cc. if you give it subcutaneously (not intravenously), so we were able to divide it up among us.

As a result of this situation we had all these typhoid cases on our ward. There was this little Jap corporal, a miserable little bastard, who used to come in there every once in a while. One day he came and saw that these typhoid cases were out of bed and sitting in chairs and on the porch. He got mad as hell, because he said they should be in bed, so he called me over and we had an interrogation with a British guy interpreting. He was no bargain at all, either. They kept asking me why I let these guys run around and sit up when they were sick. I said, "I never told them they could sit up. They just did that on their own." They kept hammering away at that. Finally this little Jap put me on the list to be shipped out of there up to Japan or up north. But then he was transferred out of the camp, and Glattly had them take my name off the transfer list. There was a Jap sergeant there who was a pretty nice fellow. He'd give Glattly and this Britisher the same food that the Japs were getting, which was much better than ours.

They had some mining in northern Formosa and they kept the prisoners working there underground until they were just physical wrecks, and then they'd ship them down to this supposed hospital that we had. When we got them they'd have edema—ascites—in their abdomen and we'd tap them, stick a needle in. They had urinary suppression; they wouldn't pass any urine, and then they'd have big bellies. So we'd stick a syringe into the abdomen to drain it. We had to be careful where we put it, because we didn't want it to go in the bladder or the diaphragm. So we'd get it in there and then drain it; once we got it drained, they'd start passing urine. It made a big difference in these guys. We'd take off gallons, really gallons of this fluid. From one of them, I remember, I took off two or three gallons of fluid.

There were a lot of rats in the camp. You could see probably twenty to thirty rats by the stream at any one time, and in our building rats were always climbing around on the walls. At night we used the mosquito bars to keep the goddamn rats away. And by then we all had beriberi, and we had to get up at night and urinate, usually about ten times a night. You wouldn't urinate in the daytime at all when you were on your feet, but at night when you were lying down, you'd have to keep getting up and go outside. One guy in our barracks also had scabies, which meant he was covered all over with this ointment. For scabies you have to cover yourself with an ointment, all except your face, for three days—it's a miserable treatment. So he had all this ointment on, and

then he kept this big can there to urinate in at night because he also had beriberi. One night the can was full,
and one of the rats bit his foot. They used to bite your
toes. Of course, it was pitch dark; we had no lights at
night. So when the rat bit him, he jumped up and the rat
got mixed up in his mosquito net, and it tipped over this
big can of urine, which spilled all over him. It was the
goddamnedest mess you ever saw.

On Formosa, the coldest it got was about 45 degrees.
But we were so emaciated from lack of food and everything that it seemed much colder. And even that was
damn chilly when you are outside all the time. The only
bathing water we had was the rain. If it rained you'd take
your clothes off and go out in the rain, soap yourself up,
and then if it stopped raining, you'd sit there covered
with soap.

The Japs issued us cotton blankets. In addition, I had
two good wool blankets. So I'd pile all these blankets on,
and I'd sleep in my clothes. I had one of those aviator
helmets that went down over your ears; I kept that thing
on. And then I had a pea jacket that I'd traded for some
cigarettes a while back, and I kept that on. I'd pile up
these blankets—two Navy blankets, two wool ones—and
then I had about five or six other blankets that I'd pile on
top of that. It took me about ten minutes to get settled.
So I'd finally get set, but within about half an hour I'd
have to get up because of the beriberi. You'd have to go
about every half hour all night long. Your sleep was, you
might say, pretty well broken up.

I had diarrhea one time, and to clear it up I took a
dose of castor oil. It sounds almost unbelievable, but I
got up twenty-four times that night to go to the bath-
room, which was outside the building. The next day I
was really all in. Colonel Glattly came over, and he said,
"I understand you're feeling kind of sick, Bill."

"Well," I said, "I've had this goddamned diarrhea all night, twenty-four times."

"Take one of these pills," he said, and he gave me some phenobarbital, and that was the end of it.

The morale was better up on Formosa. In Bilibid, the morale was terrible. It was very low. But in Taiwan the morale was much better. The one pleasant time during the whole prison period, as I think back, was on the ship in the Hong Kong harbor; the weather was perfect and we slept on deck.

Luckily, the weather on Formosa wasn't too bad. Some of the prisoners were up in Siberia; my friend John Breslin ended up there, and he said it got to 10 to 20 degrees below zero. They had no heated buildings, and he said they just about froze. He said they'd burn everything—desks and chairs—anything just to keep a fire going. Then they'd get as close to the fire as they could. He said they suffered a lot. At least, we didn't have anything like that.

We had heard that the Japs planned to kill all the prisoners before they surrendered. On the ship one of the Japs got very friendly one time and he invited a couple of us officers up there to have supper with him on the upper deck. He said, "Most of these prisoners will be killed before this thing is over. But," he said to a couple of us, "I'll save you." He said they're going to put all the prisoners in a cave and in front of the cave they'll have machine guns, and if you try to get out you'll get machine-gunned.

Toward the end of the war prisoners were getting increasingly sick from malnutrition. Of course, there was a lot of malaria. I had had malaria earlier but I treated it, as I said, and got over it. Colonel Glattly had his headquarters—about two or three rooms there—in a little shack, and in the main room he had a teapot that was on all the time. We used to go over there to get a drink of tea. He also had a great big box measuring about two by three feet, about four feet high, a box of brewer's yeast powder, which they called Ebios. I knew this yeast stuff was very valuable for us; it was pure vitamin B. We could help ourselves to it, so every night before we ate, we'd get a whole big dish full of this Ebios. Lewis particularly was crazy about it, so Al Poweleit used to call him the Ebios Kid. One of us would go over there every night and put it on our rice. It'd make the rice much more palatable and it was also extremely valuable; I think that did us a hell of a lot of good. The sick didn't like the taste of it, though; they wouldn't eat it.[4] I began to get rid of a lot of edema that I had had in my legs. When we finally arrived in Taiwan, after thirty-nine days on that ship, my legs were all swollen up because of beriberi. This also happened to the other officers. So the brewer's yeast helped reduce the effects of the beriberi.

We also had a lot of medicines there that had been sent from the States. They sent a Red Cross ship over, and the Japs had stored these valuable vitamins in a cave. But Glattly and his British aide wouldn't give any of it to the Americans. They would just give it to the very sick prisoners, the ones that weren't going to live anyway. Glattly said he was trying to save it. I don't know what the hell he was trying to save it for. This British aide was kind of a snoop, always sticking his nose into other people's business. So we were trying to get some of these vitamins; he kept them in a tunnel. One day, Poweleit, Lewis, and I went into the tunnel and helped ourselves to the vitamins. Of course, the Britisher came sneaking in and saw us there and ran right back and told Glattly.

So then we went and spoke with Glattly. I said, "You know we're in fairly decent shape. Most of these guys with ascites are swollen all over, there's nothing that's going to bring them back. They're beyond the point of no return. We're still in pretty good shape. I've got a wife and daughter back there, and I don't want to go back blind and a physical wreck. I've got a long life ahead of me. We think this Ebios is very valuable." Well, he kind of accepted that. We said, "You know, you talk about us getting this brewer's yeast, but you get a full meal every night. We've seen the Japs carry you over two trays. You get the same food that they do. We don't get that. You do, you and that Britisher."

"Bill," he said, "we don't have any choice. They just give it to us. They won't give it to anybody else. We can either take it or turn it down. So, rather than waste it, we take it."

"Well," we said, "it doesn't look good for you two to be eating good meals while everybody else is starving. It just doesn't look good."

For Christmas in 1944 the British put on a nice skit. The Japs gave us some extra food. They killed a horse, so we had some horse meat, and we all sat down at this table in a circle. The senior British officer gave a nice little talk, and then after dinner, at noon, they had a play that they all put on, and we all went over to that. It was quite an enjoyable break. As in Bilibid occasionally there would be a Jap holiday—a "*yasume* day"—and they'd give us some beer, or *caki*, these awful cakes. They seem to have a lot of holidays.

But if they'd get some bad news—for instance, when the U.S. bombed Tokyo and practically burned the city to the ground—then they were nasty as hell to us. There was one Jap there that was sort of crazy. He had gotten some bad news about Tokyo being bombed, and he took six prisoners over to one side of our compound and made them dig graves for themselves. Then they had to get down on their knees and stick their heads out. They had their hands tied behind them. He stood over them with his saber, as if he were going to cut their heads off. He stood that way for about an hour, or an hour and a half, and then he let them go. Then he went up to their headquarters, and when he came back he handed us a bottle of gin and apologized. He said, "I don't know. Something happens up here," and pointed to his head. He was kind of apologizing for the rampage he'd gone on.

We used to trick the Japs sometimes, though. One time we had this Jap guard who asked if I would take his blood pressure. A British captain who worked with me realized he could take advantage of this, so he made a great big chart, and he put this guy's blood pressure way up at the top, and he said to me, "How long do you think this war is going to last?" I said, "It's going to last at least six months." Every time this guy would come in, he'd give us cigarettes. So I started him off saying his blood pressure was about 250 over 150 or so, and we'd give him some of these gray pills. I didn't know what they were for, but I said, "Oh, those are good for your blood pressure." So he took them. He'd come in every few days; actually we'd round him up. This captain would go out and get him, and say, "You've got to come in and get your pressure taken," and he'd put it at 145 or 135 or something and we gradually ran it down. We figured we had this guy for at least six months' worth of cigarettes.

One time a captain and I were up in one of the shacks, and there was a guard who walked by all the time. The captain had a disposable razor blade that he'd been sharpening on the leather of his shoe. The blade was about three years old. He put it on his razor and then the Jap guard walked by and he showed him the blade. The guard decided he wanted that blade, so he sold it to him for a pack of cigarettes. I had an automatic lead pencil, and the guard wanted that pencil in the worst way. So he bought it for a pack of cigarettes. Then he came back, and he said, "It doesn't write." (I had taken all of the lead out of it.) "Oh," I said, "the leads are extra, you got to pay extra for those." So I sold him a piece of lead. I had all this lead, and he began buying the lead so his pencil would write. That kept me in cigarettes for a while.

Finally the war in Germany ended in May of 1945, and the Japs had to admit that they were fighting a war by themselves. It was just a question of time how long they would hold out. Then we dropped the atomic bombs, one on Hiroshima and one on Nagasaki, and that gave the Japs a good excuse to surrender. They thought we were going to drop one on the emperor, so they surrendered, and MacArthur took the formal surrender on the second of September 1945. I was on Taiwan. We had a radio. We listened to the surrender ceremony."

Notes

1. Captain Donovan (then a lieutenant colonel) mentions this in a War Claims application filed in 1953. (Pursuant to the War Claims Act of 1948, as amended 1952, former POWs who received "inhumane treatment," as defined by the 1929 Geneva Convention, were to be compensated by the U.S. government at the rate of $1.50 for each day of such treatment.)

2. Daws, *Prisoners of the Japanese*, 325.

3. E. Bartlett Kerr, *Surrender and Survival: The Experience of American POWs in the Pacific, 1941–45* (New York: William Morrow, 1985), Appendix C.

4. This incident is recounted in Poweleit, *USAFFE*, 129, as follows: "Captain Donovan obtained some Ebios (Vitamin-B powder) and we put this on our rice. Captain Lewis, Royal Medical Corps, asked why they didn't give all the Ebios out to the men instead of trying to save it for a future time. I was in perfect agreement with him."

7

Coming Home

CAPTAIN DONOVAN WAS EVACUATED by plane to the Philippines from Taihoku, Taiwan, on September 6, 1945. The next day he cabled and wrote to his wife and family—the first that they had heard from him directly since the form cards that he had sent from Camp #8 eighteen months previously. (My mother had received two of these cards as late as January 15 and 22, 1945.) He, however, received no word from them. Even though they sent many cables and letters, none got through to him. As his cables to them became more and more frantic, asking for news from home, my mother, finally in desperation, contacted various public officials hoping to be able to access official communication lines. Eventually, my father heard from her, learning that all was well, just before his departure from Manila on September 18 abroad the USS *Hugh Rodman*. After a short stay in San Francisco my father proceeded across country by train, meeting my mother and me in Chicago on October 9, 1945.

I remember the day well. The train was due in at Union Station at 8 A.M. My mother had me smartly dressed up, complete with white gloves. Soon after we arrived at the station, however, we were told that the train would be several hours late. I recall my mother's anxious face at the information booth. The station was, of course, bustling with returning soldiers and sailors in uniform and their welcoming families. We returned to the hotel, the Palmer House, where my mother put a fresh set of gloves on me—I had been dragging my hand against the sooty walls of the station—and washed the dirty pair. We repeated this trip several times during the day, as the train was reported delayed many times. Finally, around 5 P.M. my father's train came in. I recall that my mother suddenly began to run and that she bumped into someone. I continued on a few steps and then realized that she had remained bumped. I looked up and there was my father. The next day the three of us went up to Madison for a family reunion. We stayed there for six weeks and then went back to New York.

"About a week after V-J Day, we learned that the war was over when in the camp on Formosa the Japs called us together and said that the United States and Japan were going to be "friends" again now and that we were free. They said, "The United States and Japan have decided to be friends again, and so you are no longer prisoners." They recommended, however, that we keep the guards there in protection from the local people of Taiwan, the so-called savages, who were uncivilized people who lived up in the mountains. So we kept the guards, but we were free to go wherever we wanted.

There was no reaction to the news. You'd think there'd have been a lot of cheering, but there wasn't. People were numb. However, we did decide to sing the national anthem. The Dutch started out and sang theirs. Then we were going to sing "America" because it's easier than "The Star Spangled Banner." But the British sang their "God Save the King." So that left us with "The Star Spangled Banner." Well, none of us could figure out how to sing it—it's the damnedest song to sing—so about three of us tried to sing it. We couldn't remember half the words. It wasn't a very good rendition.

After V-J Day they sent planes over with Red Cross bags of supplies. Some of them had food; some had clothing; some had type O blood. They were supposed to parachute them down, but the ropes weren't strong enough and they'd break loose from the parachute and then come crashing down. So anytime you saw these planes coming over dropping these things, you'd run and get the hell out of the way, because if you ever got hit by one of those, you'd be a goner. One of them, in fact, hit a Chinaman standing right outside the camp, and that was the end of him. So when you saw these so-called relief supplies coming, you'd try to get the hell out of the way.

The first American that we saw was a captain who came into the camp the same day as the surrender on the battleship *Missouri*. As I say, MacArthur took the surrender there in Tokyo Bay, and we heard it by radio. This captain seemed like a giant. I later ran into him in the Pentagon, and he wasn't a large fellow at all. He was just very average size, probably about five foot eight, but he had seemed so large out there. The captain had been over in China. He told us quite a bit about the war. He told us how the Germans had persecuted the Jews. He said what we went through was nothing compared to what they did.

Then they put us on a train and sent us up to Taihoku in Formosa. A U.S. aircraft carrier arrived shortly and our group of POWs all left, except for Captain Poweleit and myself, the two doctors. We had to stay behind because we had about twenty patients. Colonel Glattly, the commanding officer, said that as soon as we had adequate help for the patients, we could leave. The aircraft carrier had just barely got out of sight when in came about six or eight British doctors on a British hospital ship, and we quickly acquainted them with the patients.

There was one patient there, a young guy by the name of Pyle, who had been a striker. A striker is a guy an officer will hire, paying him a little extra, to keep his uniforms clean or do little tasks. This Pyle was in pretty poor shape physically; Poweleit and I used to give him a little extra food and gave him practically nothing to do. We gave him a little money too. But after we left, I found out later—I talked to his mother—that he had died on the way back. As a matter of fact, the treatment had killed him, because when they are so weak, you can't feed them too much. They found that out in various places—in Africa, for example. One thing they can take is milk. You've got to just gradually wean them—bring them back their strength gradually. This hospital ship came in and they immediately started pouring food into Pyle, and also giving him transfusions, and it just killed him. He would have lived if we'd have taken care of him. We went to see him when we were leaving. Poweleit and I stopped by to say good-bye. He was very short of breath then, where he hadn't been at all before, and they had blood going into him. They didn't know how to treat him.

There were two planes at the airport at Taihoku—DC-3s that were flown up from the Philippines. They were flying back right away. I asked a pilot if we could go aboard. He was a young fellow, about eighteen or nineteen. He said, "Sure, come on in." Then I said to Poweleit, "Let's load these patients up on this plane, and get the hell out of here." "Well," he said, "I'm going to stay until tomorrow." Why he wanted to stay is beyond me. I wanted to get back to U.S. territory. I knew the sooner I got back to U.S. territory, the better I would feel.

On the way to the planes another incident occurred. We were driving in a truck driven by a U.S. major, and there was a Jap officer walking alongside. He had a samurai sword. We picked him up and asked him if he wanted a ride, and he said, "Yeah, sure." We were going along about forty or fifty miles an hour, and the major said, "Let me look at your sword." So he looked at it, and then he gives the Jap a shove and he says, "Good-bye!" The Jap flopped out of the truck and landed on the road and rolled around for a while and then he finally got up. We were just arriving at the airport. The airport was surrounded by about ten thousand Jap soldiers, and a lot of them didn't even know the war was over. This Jap came running after us, shaking his fists and yelling. So the major turned to me and he said, "What the hell are we going to do now?" I said, "Give him his goddamn sword!" So he threw the thing out on the road, and the Jap picked it up and dusted it off, and started walking along peacefully. We arrived at the airport and loaded up the patients on the plane. I took about half of the patients and Poweleit was going to take the other half the next day. Those that weren't well enough to travel by air were going to go back by ship.

The young pilot flew us down to the Philippines. It was September 6, 1945. That was a hell of a long day for me. We got up about four in the morning. Somebody had a bottle of whiskey, and we distributed that; we drank that up first for breakfast. Then we flew back to Manila. The pilot flew very low. A lot of the Japs didn't know that the war was over, and so our pilots didn't fly up high where they could get hit. It took just a few hours, as opposed to the thirty-nine days getting up there on the ship. I thought we were going to hit the waves, we were so close to the water; we were just barely skimming over it. We flew over Manila harbor, and was that lit up! God, I never saw so many lights from all these ships. It was like daylight! The harbor, Manila Bay, was just full of ships.

We landed at Nichols Field. It was the busiest airport in the world right then, with planes coming in every few seconds. It was about midnight when I got out of the plane. It was a strange feeling to be free again. I had been a prisoner for about three and a half years. Soon after I arrived I cabled Dode in the States, which was the first she had heard from me directly in eighteen months.

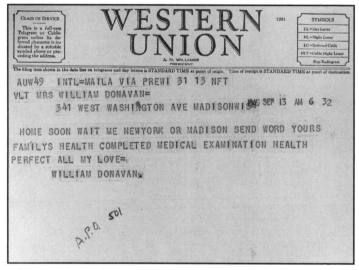

Cable received in Madison, September 13, 1945, announcing Captain Donovan's liberation and return to U.S. custody in Manila.

The Red Cross had set up a place where each prisoner was allowed to send a cable. I sent several actually, but I never got any back. There was this moron who would read off the names for mail call. He would say things like "Here's one, this fellow, this prisoner got back and found that his wife had divorced him. She's married somebody else and they live over in Hong Kong now." Then he'd laugh, he'd laugh like hell. Well, I didn't think it was funny. I hadn't heard anything from Dode. I didn't know if they were still alive. So I began sending telegrams. I finally even sent one down to Tony [his brother] in Peru, and Tony called them up in Madison and said, "For God's sake, send Bill a cable. Tell him that you're still alive, at least." Eventually, just before we sailed back to the U.S., I got a letter from Dode, dated August 5, 1945, and then I got a cable aboard the ship.

The surgeon for the Far East, Col. Wibb Cooper, who had been the senior medical officer on Corregidor, came up to us at the airport and asked me about Colonel Duckworth and some of his friends. Then he said, "I'll be back in a little while to get you." They sent a bunch of ambulances for us. We were a mixture of prisoners; some were Dutch, and some were British, and some were God knows what all, and they all went to different hospitals. So we started off. I was in one of these ambulances. They dropped off the Dutch and the British and they finally got to the last hospital and they dropped me off, and then they left.

They still had a blackout going, so I was standing there. I had been up since four o'clock in the morning and this was after midnight. God, I was tired. A captain, who was O.D. [Officer of the Day], came out and said, "What the hell do you want?"

"I want a place to sleep."

"I'll have to ask the C.O.," he said. He didn't seem to realize that I was one of the released POWs that the ambulance had just brought in. So he went off and when he returned he said, "You can stay here tonight, but then you've got to get the hell out of here the first thing in the morning. The C.O. doesn't like stragglers around here." I was a straggler! So I went in and fell asleep. About nine o'clock the next morning, Colonel Cooper showed up. He said, "I've been looking all over for you. I didn't know where the hell you had gone last night. I have been looking for you for the last two or three hours." He said, "Come on with me," and then he took me someplace and got me a good breakfast. Then he put me in a tent camp that they had just outside of Manila. You had to stay there and wait for transportation home. As POWs we had priority, but a lot of them had to wait as much as six months to get back.

While we were waiting, they set up a special diet for the POWs. We walked through the mess in a special line. On one side was the regular line and on the other side was the special food, a lot of fruits and stuff that ordinarily they didn't have, and we could have what we wanted there. They also set up a shack where you could have all the free drinks that you wanted, including beer. So you could sit there in the evening and have a glass of beer. They also issued us new uniforms. I got a very good uniform, but it was a size 37. My ordinary size was a size 40–42 or even as much as 44. I was down to 135 pounds, but I gained weight rapidly so that I was more or less normal by the time I got back to the United States. We could have gone by plane, but the planes were old and they were having a lot of bad luck, a lot of crashes. Practically all of us decided to go back by ship.

They sent all of these entertainers over too, and I remember sitting there at night and they'd have a hell of a good band playing a lot of good music, which we hadn't heard for a long time. Then they'd present little plays. This was all outside, and as far as mosquitoes, DDT had been introduced, and you would spray that around and there would be no mosquitoes anywhere. It was very noticeable. When you slept in a tent, you would spray this DDT around a little bit and then go to sleep, and you didn't need a mosquito bar or anything. There were no mosquitoes at all.

Manila had been virtually destroyed. The Jap general had decided to fight for the city after MacArthur landed at Lingayen Gulf. Eisenhower said that the destruction of Manila was worse than any city in Europe. There was nothing standing. You couldn't orient yourself, because there were no landmarks. Everything was leveled. God knows how many Filipinos were killed.

Meanwhile, my friend Waterous, who had been in Bilibid, was having a continuous party at his place. It went on twenty-four hours a day. They sat there telling stories—mostly these were submarine commanders. They were interesting to talk to. I told them about the radar pings we heard hitting the sides of the prison ship. Sometimes they'd go up to Baguio, a resort up in the mountains that Dode and I had gone to before the war. Waterous had a place up there. They'd move the party up to Baguio, then they'd stay there a while, and then they'd come back. He also had a place on an island just south of Luzon.

In Bilibid we'd had a priest that most everybody hated. He wore a captain's insignia, although he wasn't a captain. He was a lieutenant. He used to go into Manila and pick up all kinds of food and then he'd keep it for himself. The Filipinos would give it to him for the prisoners, but this guy would keep it for himself. He would sit there eating like a hog. Only rarely did he invite anyone over for dinner or breakfast. He would have bacon, eggs, and, God, everything you could think of. The Navy, oh, how they hated him! And Waterous hated him. Waterous said if he ever met him in the street after the war, he was just going to smash him in the face, without any words. He said he was just going to wallop him.

I stopped and visited Waterous several times before we left for the States. He'd take me up to this auditorium he had, and he'd say, "Well, what movie do you want to see?" Then we'd start to watch a movie. Usually we'd watch only a little of it, then turn it off, because we'd rather talk. Finally, the night before I left the Philippines, I stopped to say good-bye to him, and he had gardenias in his yard. They grew around there like dandelions do around here. He picked one and said, "Take this home and give it to your wife when you get home. Tell her I sent it to her." I corresponded with Waterous after the war for quite a while, until he died. He didn't live that long, though. He had a bleeding hiatal hernia.

Finally, we got on our ship to go back. I was in a cabin where they did nothing but play poker. They played poker every night all night long. They'd start right after supper and they'd break up at sunrise. And the guy in the bunk above me, who had been a POW, did nothing but talk constantly, just yak. He always had his head hanging over the side talking and yelling. All I wanted was quiet. I wanted to sleep. I was so damn glad to get all of this over. So I told my friend Breslin, who was also on this ship, and he said, "Why don't you come with us? We've got a great big room and there's only two of us, and it's a room that could hold about ten or twelve." So I moved all my stuff in there with them, and it was nice and peaceful from that point on. I came back the rest of the way in that. It was a pretty pleasant trip, really. I had some very good friends on the ship, and, of course, the food was wonderful compared to what we had been having.

It took fifteen days. The captain was supposed to stop in Hawaii but decided to skip it. We went up and talked to him, Breslin and I. He said, "I can see why we won this war, when I meet you prisoners, but the class of men that we've been hauling around up until now, they were the worst bunch that you'd ever imagine." He skipped Hawaii and went straight on to San Francisco. Going under that Golden Gate bridge was quite a feeling—to come under that bridge, you feel like you are back home. We landed there at the Presidio on October 3, 1945.

I called Dode from San Francisco. Just as I was going into the phone booth I ran into the dental officer that I had last seen on Bataan during the evacuation to Corregidor, the one who cleared the way. I told him we never would have made it without him; he did a hell of a fine job. I called Dode two or three times. The first time I told her I was on my way back. Until my cables from Manila had arrived in September she hadn't heard from me in about eighteen months. They didn't know what had happened to me. They knew some of the prison ships had been sunk, and that I had been on a prison ship, but as far as they knew, I wasn't on any of the ships that were sunk. They had heard this from Colonel Craig, who was a POW there in Bilibid, and he'd kept track of those ships. Right after the war he contacted my wife and told her that I was okay. Then there was that man from Wisconsin, Avery Wilbur, who had survived the sinking; he knew me. He had talked to Dode and said that he was quite sure that I was not on any of the ships that were sunk. He said I was on a different ship.

Some very good friends, Colonel and Mrs. Weiss— he had been my commanding officer down at Fort Moultrie, South Carolina, before the war—had come down to meet the ship, but they missed me somehow. So they took us to Letterman Hospital. The chief of medicine there said, "I'm not going to admit you to the hospital now, but if you're going to leave overnight, sign out. Let us know where you are. Because you'll be here for a few days. We're not prepared to do any definitive treatment or diagnosis here."

I decided to telephone the Weisses. They were at San Mateo, which is a few miles from San Francisco. They immediately invited me out there, and said they had been trying to contact me. I went out by streetcar. They had a beautiful little house there. They couldn't have been nicer, the both of them. I stayed there for several days. The colonel had a great big new Packard, and every morning he'd take me for a ride. He showed me the whole area around San Francisco.

I stayed with the Weisses there in California for several days, waiting for a train back East. I went down there on a Tuesday or a Wednesday, and on Friday they said, "Stay over for the weekend!" But on Saturday around noon my friend Breslin called and said, "We're leaving at six tonight; the train is pulling out at six."

"Take all my clothes and everything that I have," I said, "and put it in a big box and put it in line there, will you?"

He said, "Okay, I'll do that."

Weiss took me to the depot, and I went back in to San Francisco by train. I went up to the headquarters, because I still had to get a ticket. At headquarters there was a WAC just leaving, and she said, "You're too late. You have to get a ticket and you have to do this and that. The train is leaving at six." So I started to leave, but she said, "You really want to be on that train, don't you."

"I sure do," I said. "I haven't seen my wife in five years, four and a half to five years!"

"Well, I'll give you a car and driver. Can you pay for the tickets? You'll be reimbursed for them later. Do you have money enough to buy tickets to get you to Madison?"

I said that I did, so she gave me a car and driver and we had to go over to some other place to get the tickets. The train didn't leave from San Francisco; it left from one of those little towns across the big bridge. I went out and got the tickets and came back, and then she took me to the depot, and we got there in time.

Just a few minutes before the train left an ambulance came whooshing up and out of the ambulance came Colonel Glattly. He had been at a football game up in northern California. They called for him on a loud-speaker at the game and told him this train was leaving at six. Finally we got on the train.

I had called Dode once, and I called her again on the way back. I think it was just after we passed Salt Lake City. I called her about two in the morning. When I got back to the depot, the train I'd been on was nowhere in sight and I thought, "My God, I missed the train!" Then I noticed a car sitting over at the side; it was the car that we were on. They had a special car for POWs and it had all kinds of food and everything. All the way back from San Francisco to Chicago, every time they'd stop, women in the towns there would have sandwiches. They'd have pheasant sandwiches—everything you can imagine—a big spread there, all kinds of food, wonderful food. In addition, they had a special WAC there who was supposed to give us anything we wanted. They had a special car that had a shower in it, and we all took a shower. We had all the liquor we wanted, too, although we didn't drink much of anything. A drink would really affect you. When you're so run down, drinks go right to your head, especially up at an altitude. When we were crossing the Rocky Mountains up there in Wyoming, we all went in and had a couple of drinks and they went right to our heads.

Finally we arrived in Chicago. It was about five or six at night on October 9. Dode and Josie were there. Dode had taken Josie. The train was supposed to have been in at eight in the morning. There were five sections to this particular train. There was a train every ten minutes all the way from San Francisco. Dode had taken Josie back to the hotel about five times to change her clothes, she got them so dirty. But finally I was reunited with Dode, and I picked Josie up and threw her up in the air. Dode said, "You couldn't have done anything better; that's what she likes." Then we went to the hotel. Joe [his brother] had gotten me a reservation at the Palmer House, one of the best hotels in Chicago, and we spent the night there. Just before we put Josie to bed, she said, "You be here in the morning. When we get up, if you're not here, I'll be mad." She was afraid I would disappear again. The next morning I took Josie for a little walk, and she was looking for a subway. I guess she thought she was in New York. As far as I knew there were no subways in Chicago. We were at the corner of Michigan Avenue, and Josie was pulling one way, and I was pulling the other way, and I thought, "If a cop sees us, he'll think I'm trying to kidnap her." I finally got her to walk past the hotel where we had been staying and I pushed her through the revolving doors and got her back in.

We planned to stay in Chicago for a couple of days, but I was a little afraid they were going to have a big delegation out to meet us in Madison and I didn't want that. I had been pretty well publicized during the war and I was afraid they'd have some sort of ceremony. I wanted to arrive incognito. So we arrived in Madison on October 11, a day before we were supposed to. When I walked into the house, 341 West Washington, my mother and Elly [his sister-in-law] just about fell over. My mother was cleaning the house up. She had a rag around her head. Then Joe came home from work and we had a big reunion.

Several weeks later we went on to New York and stayed with Dode's mother at her apartment at 25 East 9th Street. One day in late November or early December I took Josie down to Washington Square, which was just a few blocks away; it had a playground—swings and sandboxes. As we were walking down Fifth Avenue between 9th and 8th Streets toward the square I noticed a tall woman coming toward us. I looked again and I realized it was Eleanor Roosevelt. She lived around there at that time. I was in uniform so I saluted her. She smiled and nodded and, as she passed by, she said, "Welcome home, Major." "

8

The Home Front

My mother, Josephine Devigne Donovan (Dode), and I, then an infant of two months, left the Philippines aboard the USAT *Washington* on May 14, 1941. Because of the increasing likelihood of war with Japan, the War Department on April 23 ordered dependents (as wives and children were then called) of American military personnel in the Philippines to return to the States, terming the situation a "public emergency" (War Department radiogram, April 25, 1941).[1]

Sixteen days later, including a stopover in Honolulu, we arrived in San Francisco. As my father later remarked in a letter to my mother, "The trip must have been a nightmare from what you said and from what some of the other wives wrote to their husbands" (letter of June 11, 1941). It is easy to reconstruct that a two-week sea voyage and a cross-country train trip with a nursing infant would be difficult at best and, under the stressful emotional circumstances, was indeed a nightmare.

After arriving in San Francisco on May 30, my mother and I took a train that evening by way of Chicago to Madison. A week later we continued by train to New York, arriving at Pennsylvania Station on June 7. We spent the war years in New York with my maternal grandmother, Henrietta Campbell Devigne, in her six-room apartment in Greenwich Village near Washington Square. The apartment was on the seventh floor overlooking

University Place. The rent was $125 a month. Every summer from 1942 to 1945 my mother and I spent about a month in Madison.

Dode and Josie, 1943, a photo received in prison camp and carried by the author throughout his captivity.

My mother's principal occupations during the war were to raise and take care of a young child, attempt to communicate with and obtain information about my father, and work in war-relief activities. Once a week she worked as a Red Cross volunteer, folding bandages and preparing packages for the troops abroad. In a September 26, 1945, letter to my father written shortly after his liberation, my mother noted, "I did some Red Cross work packing POW food parcels[,] millions of them; I guess they helped the prisoners of the Germans, but I know very few reached you; and to think you were supposed to get one each week!" In addition, she donated seven pints of blood during the course of the war. My grandmother also worked in war relief at the Maple Leaf Society.

During the six-month period from my mother's departure in mid-May of 1941 until the attack on Pearl Harbor on December 7, my father wrote thirty-one (extant) letters to my mother, most of them timed to leave on the weekly airmail "Clipper Ship" packet. At best it took over a week for mail from Manila to reach New York, and as censorship increased by late summer, it often took a couple of weeks. Moreover, the clipper planes did not fly in bad weather. These letters were supplemented by occasional cables or "radiograms." My mother undoubtedly wrote an equivalent volume of letters to my father, but all but two of these have been lost. Like him she was attentive to the Clipper Ship schedule. In a letter dated November 5 [1941] she comments, "I see where they are holding up the China Clipper 2 days in Hong Kong to bring that special Japanese emissary to the U.S. The idea of delaying our mail! How I wish something would come of it though." The prewar negotiations my mother alludes to, of course, did not succeed. The emissary she refers to is Saburo Kurusu, who came to the United States on November 15, 1941, as a special envoy from Hirohito. On November 20 he and the Japanese ambassador, Nomuru, presented Japan's proposals to Cordell Hull, U.S. Secretary of State. The U.S. counterproposals were presented on November 26; the same day, the Japanese fleet left for Pearl Harbor.

From the extant letters it is clear that my parents kept hoping through the summer of 1941 that their separation was going to be but a temporary one; rumors repeatedly surfaced that certain officers were going to be reassigned to the States within a matter of months. By November and early December, however, these hopes were fading. In his letters my father mainly asks questions about the folks at home, chats about his daily doings, gives my mother advice, and tries to cheer her up and boost her morale. He also asks for more letters and photos from her. "Your letters," he wrote, "are lifesavers" (June 18, 1941).

The following excerpted letter, dated May 30, 1941, is fairly typical:

> My darlings Dode and Josie:
> Your radiogram arrived on Tuesday, (3 days ago) and needless to say I was very happy to hear that everything had gone so well. I'm awfully glad that Josie was taking the trip so well. . . . It is a fine feeling to know that the worst of the trip is over and that from now on it should be enjoyable. I'm sure Josie will enjoy all the attention she will get from her new relatives. . . . I'm anxiously waiting for a letter from you telling all the details of the trip. The *Washington* arrived in Honolulu just after the Clipper left for Manila. So there should be a letter on the next one. And possibly there will be one from San Francisco.
>
> Before I get much further in this letter, I want to tell you about a persistent rumor that has been going around to the effect that almost all of the regular medical officers in the Philippines are being returned to the U.S. very shortly. Apparently there is a shortage of regular medical officers in the States, and they want to get those out of the Philippines before they

are frozen here as in the last war. It sounds too good to be true, and of course until we are on the boat on the way to the States, it won't mean anything. . . . All we can do is wait and hope that it will be true. Watch the papers for the number of medical officers ordered to the Philippines. If the rumor is true they will be sending lots and lots of medical officers out here shortly.

Out here everything has gone along as usual and there isn't anything unusual to relate. Today being Memorial Day, there were a few exercises at which General Wainwright spoke a few words. So today is somewhat of a holiday and I am writing this at home in the morning. We have an interesting series of malaria cases which I am considering writing up for a medical journal. I think these cases will be more interesting than the pneumonia cases, and I will write them up first.

We are trying out something that hasn't been done before to my knowledge, which is we are giving the men returning from Bataan a full course of treatment as though they had malaria. I'm sure this will work and when it does it should make an interesting report. The prophylactic treatment they were getting was almost of no use. Starting Monday we will get all the sick cases from the Port of Manila and from Nichols field. . . .

It's going to cost you a lot more to live than you think, Dode, so don't think about saving any for the time being. You will have lots of clothes to buy for yourself and Josie. And incidental expenses in New York are very high. I'm quite sure that the $80 I'm figuring on here will be much more than I need. So I hope to be able to send more than we planned. . . . I'm sure that we will both be able to live very comfortably on the money arrangement we have made.

It's been lonesome here without you and Josie, especially on Sundays and holidays. I sure miss rides, and walks, and everything. But I am living in the hope

of being home before very long. No matter what part
of the U.S. that I might be assigned to would be perfect. . . . Of course, this is way ahead of the story, but
it is fun to think about it. And I think it is distinctly
a possibility, expecially if things remain quiet in the
Orient. Whatever you do don't worry about me, my
darling Dode. I am very comfortable here, and I don't
like to think of you worrying about me needlessly.
Let's just live for the time when we will be together
again, and only hope that it will be soon. . . .

We heard Roosevelt's talk the other morning when
it was broadcast here. I thought it was one of best
that he has given. He left the oriental situation out of
it, with the idea, so the papers say, of not stirring up
a situation which has quieted down considerably. Japan hasn't had much to say about the talk as yet.
Roosevelt certainly didn't pull any punches, in regard
to Hitlerism. If you happen to have the *New York
Times* the day after the talk, would you wrap it up
and send it out. I'd like very much to read what they
have to say about it. The English did some good work
in sinking the *Bismarck*. However, it appears that the
battle of Crete is well on the way to be lost. I think
that England isn't worrying too much about victories
in the Mediterranean, but are rather trying to keep
going until the U.S. is either in the war or until U.S.
aid can become the deciding factor in the war. What
is the talk in New York in regards to the war? There
probably is much more excitement there than we see
in Manila where there is almost none. . . .

In later letters my father comments on various fam-
ily news. On learning, for example, that my uncle André
(Devigne) had volunteered as an air raid warden in New
York, my father reassures my mother that he thinks the
chances of an air raid in New York are "pretty slim"
(July 29, 1941). On September 24 my father notes that
there is some talk about bringing the wives back to the
Philippines, but he thinks that this is out of the question

because "Japan is . . . apt to move at a moment's notice." A more ominous sign of the deteriorating situation is the fact that on November 13, 1941, my mother's birthday, my father signed a notarized statement giving her power of attorney. On the 21st my father wrote, "Things get more upset every day."

By the end of the month it is clear that war is likely. "The situation here in the Far East has been rather tense during the last few days," my father wrote on November 30. "It is difficult to see how war can be avoided permanently. . . . When it comes, if it does, don't worry about me. The Army will be well cared for, and we will always have plenty to eat. And the other dangers are rather negligible. The big worry will be the absence of information as to my whereabouts. But no matter what happens I am sure that I will be able to get word through to you that I am all right. So let's be ready for whatever happens and make the best of it."

On December 1, one week before Pearl Harbor, in the last letter my mother was to receive from him for four months, my father wrote, "All the talk is about the war. They seem to think that it is about to begin. If it will speed up the time of my arrival home it will have its bright side." He concludes, "Some day we will be together again, my Dode, of that you may be sure."

Like most Americans, my mother heard the news of the attack on Pearl Harbor on the radio. She knew, of course, that the Philippines had been attacked the next day. Her reaction to Pearl Harbor is recorded in a letter to my father, which he never received, dated December 11, 1941:

> My darling Billy,
> Well the war has come and when it did break it certainly was a terrible shock. Of course your safety is our chief concern here and we are very anxious for

news but we realize it will be some time before things are settled enough for news to get through; I know you will manage to let us hear as soon as practicable and the President in his speech Tuesday night promised the families they would get news as soon as possible.

We heard the news of the war Sunday afternoon at 3:15 when we listened to [H. V.] Kaltenborn [a radio commentator]. About ten minutes later Joe telephoned; I spoke to him and to Ma and to Elly. Ma was very calm and like us all she is trusting in Heaven and in you to take care of yourself. Do not worry about us, darling. We are well and the country has gone to war calmly and resolutely and completely united. And you my darling try just to concentrate on your work and don't let yourself in for any unnecessary danger and never forget that Josie and I are waiting for your homecoming and even though it may be a little farther off than we first thought nevertheless it will come. . . .

Just think nine months ago [Josie] put in her noisy appearance in Manila! I understand fully now the wisdom of evacuating the women and children. The strain on the men would be terrific if their wives & children were there. It must be bad enough as it is. . . . New York goes on in its usual tempo and so far all is well. Should there be trouble do not worry. I'll see to it Josie is safe. . . . [S]o let me repeat watch out for yourself and let us trust in God that this terrible thing may end soon and that we may spend the rest of our lives in a better world generally and more specifically that we may quietly live our own private lives. . . . Such irony the peaceful message of Christmas will be this year but still that "Peace on earth to men of good will" is what we are all yearning for and living for. . . .

All my love,
your Dode

After Pearl Harbor no word was received from my father until Christmas Day, when a Western Union nightletter (cable) arrived from Manila. It read: ALL WELL TELL MA DONT WORRY TAKE CARE JOSIE DONOVAN. WILLIAM NELSON DONOVAN MCKINLEY.

My mother did not hear from him again, however, until March 28, 1942 (during the siege of Bataan), when she received another cable nightletter: ALL WELL DONT WORRY THINKING OF ALL OF YOU LOVE CAPT. W M [*sic*] DONOVAN MC. Meanwhile, she suspected from the papers that he was on Bataan, which was somewhat confirmed (he didn't specify where he was, presumably because of censorship) in a letter dated February 16, which she received on April 1. In it he said he had received her Christmas package (he picked up the briefcase at the post office on his New Year's Eve trip into Manila from Bataan), and he encouraged her to "keep a stiff upper lip and keep yourself and Josie in as good shape as possible and we'll all come out of this all right." He had increased her allotment to $183 per month (his annual pay at the time was $3,912), and he asked her to cancel the car insurance, which was not operative in the event of war anyway, and "to beef up" the life insurance policies. As in his other wartime letters, there is no mention of the military situation (because of censorship). The letter concludes, "You have all my love, Dode, for ever and ever."

While my father was hospitalized on Bataan from February 27 to March 7, he learned from a friend that there was a special plane leaving that day (March 6) for Australia. It was leaving in half an hour and had a mail pouch, so that if my father hurried he could get a letter on it. My father quickly finished up a letter he had begun on February 26, dating the second part March 6, and gave it to the friend who gave it to the pilot who carried it out to Australia. It is not clear when this letter arrived (probably on August 11, 1942, when two letters arrived, according to my grandmother's diary), but after this (or the February 16 letter, which she received on April 1) my mother heard nothing until summer. In the February 26/March 6 letter my father notes that he has received no mail from her to that point. Apparently, he did receive at least one letter with photos from her during the Bataan siege, but he received nothing on Corregidor. In fact, it would be two years before he would hear from her again.

On July 5, two months after the fall of Corregidor, my mother received a letter written from Corregidor on April 29, just a week before the surrender. This letter probably went out on the seaplane that evacuated a number of nurses from Corregidor at the end of April. Another letter written earlier, April 19, arrived on August 11, 1942. Like the former letter it concludes, "You have all my love for always."

From this point on my mother heard nothing from him until March 1943, nearly a year after my father had been taken prisoner on Corregidor. During the spring of 1942 my mother wrote him several letters (twelve are extant) addressed care of "Philippine Department, U.S. Army/Luzon, P.I." These were returned stamped "Returned to Sender/Service Suspended." In these letters my mother attempts to chat about everyday things in a cheerful manner, but the strain of not knowing his whereabouts or his condition is palpable. Excerpts from these letters, which my father never received, follow:

> Monday, March 2nd 1942
> Billy darling,
> Another week has gone by and none of the letters I've written you have been returned so some effort must be being made to get the mail through. And I do hope

it won't be long before you get news of us and maybe we will hear from you soon too. . . .

Gosh darling! won't it be Heaven when you are home again and we can enjoy one another and our Josie. I wonder if the conditions under which you are living make my letters seem awfully out of key. We know so little here about what's going on where you are that it's hard to imagine what's what. I wish I could send you things and keep hoping the time will come soon when I can hear from you. I do so wish I could help somehow. God knows it is a tremendous help to me when I begin to worry to know that you can adapt yourself to all kinds of situations, that you can take it and face whatever comes along. . . .

Ever your own Dode

P.S. Ma also says we must go on hoping for the best where you are concerned and being proud that you are under the great leader you are [MacArthur].

Monday, March 9, 1942
Bill darling
. . . I am thinking of you and hoping that somehow we may be together for Josie's second birthday. . . . I made her a cake with one candle on it (I blew it out & made the wish and I am sure you know what the wish was—it was really a prayer). . . .

Thursday, March 19, 1942
My darling
Somehow I didn't write last Monday as usual and the next day the news came out that MacArthur was in Australia. At first I felt bad about it as it seemed to us here that all would be well out with you so long as he was there; however it seems that in the long run this is for the best and certainly nobody will have the re-lief of the P.I. [Philippine Islands] as much at heart as he will. Besides it is good to know he could get away

and it gives me hope that news may get to us from you and that you may hear from us. Letters have reached this country from people on Bataan or Corregidor so I am beginning to hope that soon news will come of you. At times, darling, it seems unbearable not to know where you are and how you are.

. . . May this whole terrible struggle resolve itself as soon as possible and may we be together and able to lean on one another as we should before too long. How I wish I could do something to help you my darling and how I hope to be able to surround you with peace and comfort when you come home to try and erase as much as possible these times. . . .

. . . Bill never forget the closing sentence of your last letter. "Someday we will be together again, my Dode, of that you may be sure." I remember those words constantly. . . .

Always your Dode

During this anxious period my mother wrote to numerous officials and evacuees from the Philippines, trying to get news about my father. On March 26, 1942, she wrote Francis B. Sayre, the high commissioner to the Philippines, who had just returned to the United States after his evacuation from Corregidor. She asked him if he had any information about my father.

My dear Mr Sayre:
In June of 1938, as a member of the graduating class at Bryn Mawr College, I had the good fortune to hear your commencement address. Allow me to consider that fact as an introduction which will warrant my writing this letter.

My husband, Captain William Nelson Donovan, Medical Corps, U.S. Army, at the outbreak of the war was on duty at the Station Hospital, Fort McKinley, P.I. We have heard from him three times since then, the last message coming through on Christmas Day.

I presume that he is now on Bataan and am proud that he has an opportunity to do his share serving both his country and his fellow-officers and men; but, of course, I cannot but be anxious for my husband's safety and feel that I must try every possible means of getting news of him. Thus, having read in the newspapers of your safe return, I am turning to you in the hope that you might be able to give me some information—or tell me where I could address myself for such information—as to his state of health and as to the possibility of getting news to or from my husband.

I shall be most grateful for any knowledge or advice you would impart to me and I regret any bother this letter may cause you, trusting that you will understand the anxiety that prompted its writing.

Sincerely,
Josephine Devigne Donovan

My mother received a somewhat unsatisfactory answer from Sayre on April 1, which said that he had no news of my father and enclosed a copy of an address he had delivered on March 25, upon his return. In it he said: "For two and a half months I have been living with the American and Filipino soldiers and sailors on the Corregidor front. I have watched them under devastating shellfire—living with death. Their spirit is magnificent. Battle-scarred, smoke-stained, weary but unbeaten, they are living up to the best of American traditions."

The speech then devolves into a "rally-the-home-front" peroration:

With our boys going through the tortures of war for us here in America, can there be any doubt that we will do our utmost to match their gallantry? . . . The already bleeding Axis nations can be no match for America with her well-nigh inexhaustible natural

resources, her virile and capable and huge manpower—provided only the American people awaken
to the magnitude of the task they have undertaken
and prove themselves ready to make the necessary sac-
rifices. . . . America can and will win this war. We will
be returning to Manila and to Corregidor. We shall
drive these ruthless barbarians northward. . . . I know
that the American people will not fail.

My mother later commented that inflamed rhetoric such
as this, and such as that seen in many of MacArthur's
utterances (for example, the much-quoted comment
about the "gaunt, gray ghosts of Bataan"), were not very
comforting to those who, like herself, had loved ones in
action.

As of May 21, 1942, my mother received official no-
tification from the War Department that my father was
considered "missing in action." She would continue to
receive his pay allotment, now $203 per month, for twelve
months. If by then it was determined that he was a prisoner of war, she would receive the allotments for the
duration. Otherwise, if he were presumed dead, the pay
would end. In early August of 1942, my mother received
a brief form letter from the War Department notify-
ing her that his status was "uncertain" (letter dated August 1). That information was updated in a letter from
the War Department dated November 28, 1942, written
in response to her letter of November 24: "I regret to
inform you that this office has no information relative to
Captain Donovan other than that contained in my letter
of May 21, 1942, which stated that the War Department
will continue to carry your husband on the records as
missing in action in the Philippine Islands as of May 7,
1942," the day after the surrender on Corregidor. The
signatory, Maj. Gen. J. A. Ullio, adjutant general, sug-

gests, however, that she contact the Red Cross about trying to send him a message.

In the meantime, some news about my father's condition on Bataan and Corregidor began to reach my mother in the early summer. She mentions in a letter to him dated July 16, 1942 (but returned to sender), that "we have heard from time to time that you were well, thank God." This information had come in a series of letters from people (mainly nurses) who had been evacuated from Corregidor shortly before the surrender. In a letter dated June 26, 1942, my great-aunt Margaret (Donovan Allen), who lived in Los Angeles, wrote to say she had been able to contact Juanita Redmond, a nurse who had been evacuated by seaplane from Corregidor in a group of fifty on April 29, 1942 (she later wrote a celebrated account, *I Served on Bataan*).[2] Through a go-between Redmond had said that she had taken care of my father when he was hospitalized on Bataan for malaria and that he had received the Distinguished Service Cross. She said "that Billy [my father's family nickname] had been on field duty and had gone out in the field to bring in wounded—and because he had risked his life so often to save lives he had received the D.S.C." This presumably was the first my mother had heard that he had contracted malaria. (My father had not mentioned it in his letters from Bataan and Corregidor, assuring her to the contrary that he was in "excellent health.") She had already heard indirectly about the Distinguished Service Cross from a Lieutenant Freddie Roberts, a pilot who had been evacuated from Bataan to Australia and who in April 1942 contacted a Mrs. Tracy in Madison, who then notified the family (according to a letter from my mother dated October 4, 1945). Upon learning of the DSC my mother wrote, "I am so very proud of you darling but not at all surprised . . . as I know as well how conscientious . . . you are. I can't help but shudder when I think of the danger you were in but I am glad you could be so useful" (letter of August 12, 1942).

In a letter dated July 16, in response to her letter of June 14, a Col. George S. Clarke, another evacuee, told her that my father's name had not appeared on any casualty lists through April 8. He said, however, that the men on Bataan were "starved at the time of the surrender. They had nothing but horse or mule meat for the last 41 days of the show. Hundreds could not walk on account of beriberi." Noting that the prisoners "desperately need food, sweets, medicine, and smokes," Clarke hints that the forces on Bataan had felt betrayed at the lack of support. "[N]o single officer or man ever gave up hope that the largest, and richest nation in the world would send them help, and I, for one, do not wish to see their bitterness—if we continue to forget them." Clarke enclosed a sheet calling for a nationwide campaign to send materials to the POWs in the Philippines.

A nurse, Helen Summers, who had served on Bataan and Corregidor, wrote my mother on October 5, 1942, from Long Island, where she was recuperating. She said she had seen my father on Corregidor before she left, also mentioning the DSC.

Finally, a letter dated November 22 from another nurse, Major Florence MacDonald, chronicled in dramatic detail for my mother the incidents on Bataan for which my father was awarded the Distinguished Service Cross.

> My dear Mrs. Donovan:
> I had wished so many times to hear from you so that I could tell you a story of your heroic husband. . . .
> One day he and Fr. Carbury came over to Corregidor and I had the pleasure of meeting him. He looked

well. None of them had any extra weight. They were
telling how poor the food was and I was deeply
grieved. I also heard of what your husband did and
how he was awarded the Distinguished Service medal
for heroism. He and Fr. Carburry and some other men
all unarmed were in a first-aid station. The Japs started
machine-gunning. The place got too hot for them so
they decided to try and get back of a mango tree about
50 yards away. They had to get down flat on their
stomachs and inch their way over. The conversation
on the way over was, "Which would one miss most a
left-arm or right, a left-leg or right. Wouldn't it be
horrible to lose both," etc. The bullets were hitting
so close the dirt from where they struck bounced on
their helmets. Finally they made the tree and breathed
a sigh of relief for at least a little shelter. The doctor
looked about him and realized he had left his kit half
way over on that field they had just crossed. With the
sign of the cross on himself he flattened down on the
ground again & got the kit and started back. He was
at no time able to raise his head as the bullets were
sprinkling all around him. He was almost back when
our men stepped out of the jungle and a fierce battle
ensued. The doctor needed his kit and had it. Thanks
to his bravery in going back alone over that bullet-
sprinkled piece of ground.

I saw your husband in March. He and Fr. Carburry came over to the tunnel. They were in good
spirits but had sad stories of poor food. I was able to
get 3 jars of Kraft cheese, a jar of canned soda for hot
Cokes, 2 cartons of cigarettes, some soap, and talc
powder. I also got them 2 lbs of coffee which was the
greatest treat of all.

Did you hear from your husband since Bataan
fell? I can't understand how that could be unless he is
in Japan and they allowed him to write. They can't
get messages out of the Philippines. The Japs were
not unkind to the Navy doctors and nurses. So we
hope for fair treatment for the Army doctors and

nurses. I am so glad to be able to tell you of your husband's heroism.

I pray every day for the early deliverance of our men & nurses over there. I hear the Japs are going to give the Red Cross in Geneva the names of the civilian internees. I hope they will give the names of the Army men & women. I have over fifty letters to answer and I have been writing since noon time and now it is 9 P.M. If I could write such pleasant things to all it would be grand. Hoping and praying for the early rescues of our loved ones.

Sincerely,
F. MacDonald

Kathryn Hagen, Ken Hagen's wife and a doctor herself, also wrote my mother about the incident on Bataan, having apparently also spoken to or heard from Major MacDonald:

> Miss McDonald said that our troops were advancing in the face of a waist high firing line. Their goal was a ditch some yards ahead. The men were inching their way along on the ground. Just as they reached the ditch Bill realized he had lost his medical kit. He went back alone to get it. There were injured men in that ditch waiting for his help. The story in itself is short. But we know the minutes must have seemed hours to Bill and those who waited for him.

My mother also heard from other sister wives whom she had known in the Philippines who were sharing with her the sad experience of husbands missing in action or, later, worse. One typical letter is from Marge Wright, whose husband was in the Philippines and, like my father, missing in action. The Wrights had been next-door neighbors of my parents before the war at Fort McKinley in the Philippines. The letter was probably written in the summer of 1942.

Dearest Dody:

I read in the Army Navy Journal where Bill has been awarded the D.S.C. I know what it must mean to have had that word of him, and to have that confirmation of the wonderful job he has surely been doing all along. I was really thrilled about it. I know all the thoughts and worries that must have gone through your mind when you learned about it, but still, it is word of him and something to cling to. It's meant so much to me, Dody, to know that Bill was there to take care of Eddie if anything should happen to him. I know how quiet and sure and capable he is. Maybe that's a curious thing for me to say—that I find consolation in Bill's being where Eddie is—but I just wanted you to know.

I had one very short letter from Eddie dated February 17th. It was written from Bataan and said only that he was well and "busy." I'm sure he couldn't have picked a better word for understatement. A letter from the Red Cross advised Eddie's name hadn't been on any casualty lists for Corregidor, but if you haven't had word of Bill, you too might find consolation in the fact that they did have lists of a sort up until the 6th. And Dody, I do feel that if our boys had been missing, we would know it. I just feel that an officer would be more readily reported and missed sooner than a private would be, so would surely have been listed if anything had happened.

A letter the other day from Evelyn [Noble] said that she had heard from a friend in Washington that Maxie had been cut off from the main forces in fighting and had had to fight his way back to the main lines. He had pretty tough going. . . . She also said that she had learned that both Eddie and Maxie were Lt. Colonels now. I'm afraid that means not a thing to me, nor could it possibly mean anything to them. . . .

She learned there in San Antonio that all the captured generals had been taken to Baguio. I'm just hoping that that will mean that all the officers will be taken there. If they must be interned, it will be something if they can be where it is cool and clean anyway. I worry so much about the mental well being of the boys. I hate to think of them sitting there, when to them the job is not done, and they must surely feel that there is much they should be doing if they only could. I do hope they will allow Bill to continue to practice, and will give him the wherewithal to do it with. It will help him, and the others too, so much if he is allowed to keep busy, and surely he is needed now and will be needed in the months to come if he is just given a chance. That is one place where he certainly has it over Eddie now—for Eddie's usefulness is at an end until this is over, and how that must hurt a man to just sit.

I have the rug making bee again. Yes, I can just see you laughing at the mess I'm in. But it does help me to keep on making things for our home, and planning a bit. Only this time, I'm making the rug out of old sheets that I can beg, borrow, or steal (sounds bad, doesn't it) from most any source. I'm going to be just like those boys in colleges who let their whiskers grow until they have a winning team, I'm just going to keep adding to that darned rug until this war is over. Do you know an auditorium that needs a rug with many "loving stitches" in it?

Little Eddie is getting just like the fish stories —longer and longer. . . . How wonderful it would be if Eddie could see him. He never did receive any kind of word about the baby, you know. Doesn't know when he arrived, whether he has a son or a daughter or anything. If I could just get word to him about the baby, it would mean so much. But I do have hopes that by fall we may be allowed to send word to the boys. . . .

Loads of love,
Marge

Eddie Wright survived the war hiding in the hills. Fed and protected by local Filipinos, he was never taken prisoner.

In late March 1943 the first word my mother received that my father was alive and a prisoner of war came from an unexpected source. A series of fourteen letters and cards, dated March 19, from short-wave listeners and ham radio operators arrived in Madison, reporting a propaganda radio broadcast from Tokyo that included messages from prisoners of war. One of them, from "W. N. Donovan, Captain, Medical Corps," said: "Feeling Fine. Treatment Good. Do Not Worry. Love." My mother later commented that there was something about the wording that made her think that it was authentic.

Many of these cards and letters, which were sent from locations ranging from California to Maine, transmitted not just my father's message but also personal notes of encouragement. This kindness reflects the spirit of community that seems to have emerged on the home front during the war. It is interesting to note that most of these short-wave listeners were women.

Mrs. W. M. Donovan
341 West Washington Avenue
Madison, Wisconsin
My dear Mrs. Donovan:
I hope this letter reaches you safely. I was listening to Radio Tokio tonight by short wave in order to take down the messages from American prisoners of war in Japan. I have been doing this for the past few weeks, and I have received many letters of gratitude and appreciation from relatives in this country, telling me of the comfort my letters brought to them and hoping that I would continue to listen in to the program.

About nine messages were broadcast tonight, but the reception was rather poor and the announcer's voice faded away at the most inopportune moments, chiefly when I was trying to get a name or address. He did not spell out the names, nor did he give the names of the persons to whom the messages were broadcast.

One of the messages was from W. (M.) Donovan, Captain, Medical Corps, as follows:

"Feeling fine. Treatment good. Don't worry. Love, W. (N.) Donovan."

That is all there was, and I sincerely hope the message is genuine, even though it came in the midst of a Japanese propaganda program. I happened to tune in to this program quite accidentally one night, and when I heard names and addresses of American soldiers being read, I grabbed a notebook and took down the messages in shorthand. Because of the many letters of gratitude I have been receiving, I have been listening in nightly ever since. The messages come at 11:15 or 11:20 P.M. Pacific War Time.

I hope this tiny message will bring you comfort.

Sincerely,
(Mrs. W. L.) Cecelia McKie
[Sacramento, CA]

P.S. I noticed that messages sent during the week requested such things as razor blades, canned milk, concentrated food, shoes, socks, underwear, tobacco, books, etc., and that contact be made through either the International Red Cross in Geneva or the Information Section, Prisoners of War, Tokio, Japan. However, tonight's messages were all very brief and made no such requests.

Kin of
Captain W. M. Donovan
341 West Washington Ave.,
Madison, Wisconsin
Dear Friend:—This evening at 7:20 P.M. (East. War Time) I heard "The War Prisoner Program" from Tokyo, Japan on the short wave band of my radio. Sta-

tion JLG4 Tokyo on 15,105 K.C. A message from
Captain W. M. Donovan, U.S. Medical Corps, was
read in English by the Japanese announcer:—

He said:—"I am well and receive good treatment.
Do not worry about me. Love to all, W. M. Donovan."
(There was a bit more to the message but the radio
reception was so noisy that it was quite impossible to
hear it.)

I take this liberty in passing this information on
to you, as the Japanese announcer said the listeners
should contact the above address. I trust this information will be of value to you and may God protect
Captain Donovan and return him safely at last to his
loved ones.

Respectfully yours,
Irwin F. Bender
[Oberlin, PA]

P.S. I have written many messages (received on this
program) to dear ones at home, and I hope every lis-
tener that hears similar programs will contact the
"folks at home" for the sake of the brave men "out
there." What a pity it would be if some dear, brave
boy were to send out a message to loved ones at home
and no one would be listening to hear the precious
message and relay it to its destination!

Some of the messages were sent on form letters or
postal cards. One of them, from St. Joseph, Missouri,
was addressed to "Mrs. W. M. Bartes or Bates wife of
W. M. Bartes prisoner of war, 331 _____ Ave.,
Madison, Wisconsin," advising: "Postmaster please read
back of card." Amazingly, the mail carrier was able to
decipher this and the card was delivered. Apparently also
at least one of the listeners recorded the message and sent
the family the audio disk. In a letter to my father dated
April 24, 1943, my grandmother, Edith Nelson Donovan,
noted, "We got the short wave message you sent. It was

picked up by [censored] and they all sent word of it. Then we got a record of it this week and after having heard it ourselves on the Victrola sent it along to Dode [in New York]."

According to Gavan Daws in *Prisoners of the Japanese*, "The Japanese permitted a few prisoners to send a spoken radio message. The messages were recorded onto disks. . . . Then the approved disks were played over the Japanese shortwave propaganda stations. The message senders were chosen by lot."[3] Once they received the transmissions, short-wave radio listeners took it upon themselves to send prisoners' messages to their relatives, as those noted above did for my mother. Because of the use of form cards it is apparent that for some, relaying messages became a major operation, establishing an interesting unofficial communications network —run largely by women, it appears—that was instrumental in getting crucial information about loved ones disseminated.

The U.S. government apparently took a dim view of these propaganda broadcasts, which were part of a daily series of half-hour programs called "Humanity Calls" (later supplemented by another series, "The Postman Calls"). The program opened with an announcer saying, "This is Humanity Calls, bringing you messages from your missing men in Japanese prison camps. We know that when you hear these messages, you will help us by relaying them to those for whom they are intended. The first one today is from . . ."[4] After several messages came a musical interlude, then some propaganda, then more messages. American officials downplayed the messages, stating that there was no guarantee of authenticity. They also warned relatives against mentioning the broadcasts in letters to POWs because such letters would be rejected by U.S. censors. Nevertheless, a number of short-wave listeners, as we have seen, continued to pass on the messages, "many of which," one historian notes, "proved to be genuine."[5]

In an interview with a reporter for the *New York World-Telegram*, June 14, 1943, my mother expressed her gratitude to the short-wave listeners: "I don't hear short-wave," she said. "If it hadn't been for thoughtful strangers I'd never have known about the message." She went on to say the message struck her as genuine. "From a certain arrangement of words I'm confident it came from my husband though the Tokyo voice was speaking."

Upon receiving these cards and letters, my mother wrote on March 20 to the War Department asking for confirmation. Four days later the department informed her (although apparently not in response to her query) that the above radio message had been received but that it was "unable to verify" it, meaning that officially my father's status remained MIA. In an April 13, 1943, letter written in response to my mother's March 20 letter, General Ulio reiterated that "no official report concerning Captain Donovan had been received in the War Department. . . . Until official information is received concerning Captain Donovan's whereabouts, mail for him cannot be delivered. May I express the hope that favorable news will be available at an early date."

My mother wrote back on April 14 asking for clarification of her status vis-à-vis continuing pay allotments, which were scheduled to terminate the following month (the twelve-month anniversary of the fall of Corregidor) if my father's status were determined to be "presumed dead." In a letter dated April 22, 1943, the War Department responded: "Under Public Law 848, the Secretary of War is authorized to direct the continuance of a person's missing status beyond the expiration of twelve months, if they may reasonably be presumed to be living. On or about May 7, 1943, a review of the case of your husband will be made, and you will be informed of the results. If the missing status is continued, pay and allowances will continue to accrue and all allotments will remain in force."

On April 25, the day after my father's thirty-third birthday, my mother finally received a telegram from the War Department: YOUR HUSBAND CAPTAIN WILLIAM N DONOVAN REPORTED A PRISONER OF WAR OF THE JAPANESE GOVERNMENT IN THE PHILIPPINE ISLANDS LETTER FOLLOWS FROM PROVOST MARSHAL GENERAL ULIO THE ADJUTANT GENERAL. A follow-up letter on April 29 included a sheet of instructions about how to write to POWs.

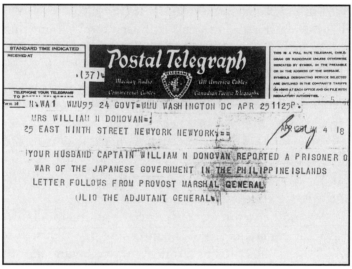

Cable received by Mrs. Donovan on April 25, 1943. Captain Donovan had been listed as Missing in Action for nearly a year.

Shortly thereafter my mother wrote to my father "In Care of the Japanese Red Cross/Tokyo, Japan" with her reaction to the news: "It is so good to be able to write you with some assurance that this will get to you. All my letters have come back to me except two [letters of April 7 and April 24, 1943] which I wrote after your message reached us last March but before we were officially advised of your status. On Easter Day, April 25th, the first official news of you came and later we received instructions on how to write you. . . . I could write pages, darling, there is so much in my heart that I want to share with you. However, these letters must be short."

In the follow-up letter, the War Department also included information about the Geneva Convention governing treatment of POWs. Given what we now know of Japanese disregard for the Geneva Convention,[6] this information is highly misleading, depicting a much rosier situation than actually existed. (Indeed, at the time the War Department knew little about conditions in Japanese POW camps.) For example, it states, "A number of reports from neutral sources indicate that American prisoners of war and civilian internees are receiving fair treatment." It also states that "current information indicates substantial compliance" with the Geneva Convention requirements that "each internment camp . . . have a properly equipped infirmary with adequate medical personnel." The sheet also notes that inspections of prison camps "are made by representatives of the Protecting Power and . . . by . . . the International Red Cross." In fact, the Japanese had not permitted inspections of the Philippine POW camps, a fact announced by the Red Cross in February 1944.[7] Finally, the information sheet claimed the Red Cross was delivering "weekly parcels to the American prisoners." In fact, only two or three of these deliveries occurred during the entire war.

The list of Japanese POWs was published in various newspapers (including the *New York Times*, June 15, 1943, and the *New York World-Telegram*, June 14, 1943, which included an accompanying picture of my father), and as a result my mother began to receive sympathy letters from several correspondents. A selection of them follows:

June 2nd 1943
349th Air Evauation Group
Bowman Field
Louisville, Kentucky
Dear Mrs. Donovan,
The news that Captain Donovan is a prisoner must have been a great relief to you. Since my friend has also been reported a prisoner, I can understand how you feel. Although it isn't the best news, at least we know they're alive. You were very fortunate to receive the message that he is well. I was also glad to hear of Major Hagen.

As you can see, I have been transferred. After a six weeks' training in this air ambulance work, I hope to have the opportunity of going overseas again. Nothing would please me more than to be present when they open the gates of those concentration camps and free our people.

Thank you for your letter—and I do hope it won't be too long before your husband is home again with you.

Sincerely,
Helen Summers

United States Senate
June 10, 1943
Mrs. William N. Donovan
341 West Washington Avenue
Madison, Wisconsin
Dear Mr.[*sic*] Donovan:
I am indeed sorry to learn through the War Department that Captain Donovan is being held as a prisoner of war by the enemy. The Department advises that you have been given all information concerning the sending of mail to him. Whenever word is received in this country regarding a change of camps, or any

other information about him, it will be immediately communicated to you. Much as I should like to be of some comfort and assistance to you, it seems that any information available to me will be sent at once to you. However, I wish to express my sympathy, and I do hope that your husband will be returned safely to you.

Sincerely yours,
[Senator] Robert M. La Follette, Jr.

Finally, on August 11, 1943, my mother received a POW form card signed by my father from Camp #3 (Bilibid). Under the heading "Imperial Japanese Army," my father underlined "excellent" among form choices following "my health is"—the other choices being "good," "fair," or "poor." (As historian Daws dryly notes, "Circling the less sunny options did not improve a man's chances that the Japanese army would forward his card."[8]) My father also underlined "uninjured" among four choices—the others being "sick in hospital," "under treatment," "not under treatment." Finally, he underlined "well" among "improving," "not improving," and "better."

In a two-line space that allowed for business messages my father asked that the adjutant general be informed that he was alive in order that allotments continue to my mother and me. And in the personal message section he wrote: "Take care of yourselves and don't worry about me, as I am all right. Much love to you and Josie and family." He concludes by sending "best regards" (the form term) to "all the family."

It is difficult to ascertain when this card was sent. E. Bartlett Kerr says that the first POW cards were mailed on January 23, 1943.[9] Commander Thomas Hayes, in *Bilibid Diary* (1987), states that prison cards were ready for mailing December 15, 1942;[10] therefore, it seems likely that they were written in late 1942, at least eight months before being delivered. POW mail was handled by the International Red Cross and transmitted by way of Geneva, Switzerland.

My mother and grandmother Donovan record the receipt of the prison card in letters to my father dated August 23, 1943, and August 26, 1943, respectively. "A postcard came quite recently from you," my mother wrote, "with your own signature at the top of it saying you were in excellent health, uninjured and well and not to worry about you as you were all right. . . . The best part of your card was your name in your own handwriting meaning that you had actually touched the card. That was the first contact I have had with you in over a year." In the same letter my mother mentions sending a Red Cross parcel.

My grandmother wrote:

August 26, 1943
Dear Billy,
It was wonderful to get that card from you with the news of you. Your handwriting was never anything to brag about but it looked beautiful in your signature. It makes us all happy to know you are well and only hope that you keep so. . . .

Much love
As ever
Mother

Between August and December of 1943 my mother received five prison cards, all except the first sent from prison Camp #8, the Ford garage camp in the port area of Manila, where my father was interned at the time, which means they were sent after February 27, 1943. The first three are limited form cards like the first, while the latter two are a bit more chatty. In one received Decem-

IMPERIAL JAPANESE ARMY

1. I am interned at—Philippine Military Prison Camp No. 8

2. My health is—excellent; ~~XXXXXXXXX~~

3. Message (50 words limit)

Hope you are all well and not worrying too much about me. Josie must be a fine little girl by now. Hope Ma, Elly, and Kids are well. Wonder where Joe, Tony, and Andre are. My love to all Devignes, Donovans. Take care of yourself and Josie. All love

Signature

William N. Donovan

IMPERIAL JAPANESE ARMY

1. I am interned at—Philippine Military Prison Camp No. 8

2. My health is—excellent: ~~XXXXXXXXXXXX~~

3. Message (50 words limit)

I hope you are all well. Would like to see snapshots of you and Josie. Give my love to Ma, Joe, Tony, Elly, the kids, and all Madison and New York folks. Just waiting for the day when I can be home with you, Josie, and all.

All my love

William N. Donovan
Signature

Received January 18, 1945

Two of the eight prisoner-of-war cards sent by Captain Donovan to his wife in 1943–44. Together with a short-wave radio message, these were the only word she had from him after the fall of Corregidor, May 6, 1942, until the liberation in early September 1945.

ber 11, 1943, he says he has sent messages "regularly," but has received only one letter, from Harold Cranefield, a friend of the family and a well-known labor lawyer. He concludes again, "Don't worry about me; am uninjured. You and Josie carry on until I return."

In another card received on December 11, my father wrote, "Dode, send this to Washington DC: To: Chief of Finance, U.S. Army" requesting that "excess money" in his account be deposited in their bank account "credit Mrs. William N. Donovan." My mother forwarded the card to the War Department on December 16, receiving a letter from the Finance Department on December 24 to the effect that there is no money "in his account" because "no payments are being made to Captain Donovan at the present time. . . . However, upon his return to the custody of the United States all pay and allowances which have accrued to his credit . . . will be paid." My mother, however, was still receiving her monthly $203 allotment.

For my mother, Christmas 1943 was a bit happier than that of 1942 because by then she had heard from my father. However, he still had received nothing from the family. The package that my mother sent in August does not seem to have arrived until March 14, 1944 (so noted in my father's handwriting on the customs declaration attached to the parcel). It may have come via the second *Gripsholm* shipment, which arrived in the Philippines in late 1943. My mother's notation on the customs declaration lists its contents:

Quantity and Description of Contents	Value
4 handkerchiefs	.95
3 socks	1.25
2 shorts (underwear)	1.50
2 shirts	7.00
1 pr shoes	5.50
1 box vitamins	4.79

14 rolls Life Savers	.70
1/4 lb. bouillon cubes	.45
nail clippers	–
pipe	–
tobacco	–
food (dried milk, dried soups, prunes)	1.55
soap [Lifebuoy]	–
playing cards	–
Total	23.69

Also included in the parcel were a letter and some photos.

Other than this parcel the only time my father received mail while a prisoner was during a four-month period from April to August in 1944, while he was in Camp #8. (My father marked the date of receipt on most of the envelopes.) There he received twenty-one letters from my mother and five from his mother written between April 1943 and March 1944.

One of my mother's letters, dated September 23, 1943, was returned by the Japanese censor along with a form sheet that stated:

> This communication is returned since the Japanese government has refused delivery of any mail to American prisoners of war and civilian internees held by Japan unless it complies with all of the following conditions:
>
> 1. Letters must be less than 25 words in length.
> 2. Letters must be typewritten or legibly block printed.
> 3. Subject matter must be strictly personal; no military or political matters or opinions may be included.
> 4. The name of the Internment Camp must appear in the forwarding address.

My mother had violated two of these newly enunci-
ated rules (no. 1 and no. 4). Up to this point her letters
had been lengthy (several, however, had gotten through).
But neither she nor the War Department knew the name
of the camp my father was in. She had from the beginning avoided mentioning military or political matters and
after receiving the War Department information in April
1943 had either typed or block-printed her letters. In a
letter written after my father was repatriated, my mother
indicated her dislike of the restraints censorship imposed.
After the censored letter was returned, my mother wrote
only short (twenty-five-word-maximum) notes. There are
eleven of these extant. Thus, altogether my father received
thirty items of mail (letters, notes, a radiogram, and a
parcel) while a POW.

A few excerpts follow from the longer letters written
by my mother before the September 1943 censorship rules
were put in effect:

> 25 East 9th Street
> New York 3, New York
> June 2, 1943
> My own darling Bill,
> . . . We went to the Central Park Zoo a few days ago;
> [Josie's] eyes almost popped out of her head when she
> saw the monkeys and her favorites were the brown
> bears. She had a ride on the pony cart and ate some
> ice cream and had a balloon. . . . As always I wished
> for you. There is so much I want to know and so much
> I have to tell you; it will be so wonderful when we
> may talk together again and share all our thoughts
> once more. Who knows? It may not be so long till we
> are together and our dreams are materializing. . . .
>
> Your own wife,
> Dode

341 West Washington Ave.
Madison, Wisconsin
July 6, 1943
My own darling Bill,

. . . Everything here is the same as ever, the only noticeable change being the vegetable garden in the rear where they are raising tomatoes and beans. . . .

I like it here because I have been here with you and everything is alive with memories of you. . . . I am living for the day when you will be [here] with us; I believe that day may not be too far off. I often wonder where and when but I do know this[,] it will be the day of days of my life.

. . . It is so strange not to have any idea of what you are doing. . . .

Ever your Dode

My grandmother Donovan informed my father in her letter of April 24, 1943, that "the St. Louis Cards. won last year's world series. They beat the Yanks. . . . All this may be ancient history to you but you see I don't know how much news you have of us."

In a prisoner-of-war card written sometime in 1944 (before October 1), which my mother didn't receive until January 15, 1945, my father acknowledged his receipt of the parcel and letters—the first he had heard from her in over two years. In his card he wrote: "Very happy that you, Ma, and all are well. Josie lovely girl. Parcel perfect and so appreciated. Deepest sympathy Mother [my father had just learned of the death on December 13, 1942, of my grandfather, Henri Devigne]. Love to Ma, Elly, the kids, Joe, Tony, Mother, and all. Living for the day when we will be together."

For my mother, however, Christmas 1943 marked a short reprieve; the darkest days of the war for her were about to begin. In January the *New York Times*, picking up a story from the *Chicago Tribune*, printed a report of Japanese atrocities on Bataan and Corregidor. It was the first time that such information had reached the American public.[11] (My mother, of course, living in New York, read the *Times* daily.) The story was based on a report made to General MacArthur and President Roosevelt by an American captain, William E. Dyess, who had escaped from Davao Prison Camp on Mindanao on April 4, 1943. Dyess, one of three officers to escape, had been on the Bataan Death March, and his report, once issued to the press, "created a sensation in the United States."[12] The information was, in fact, withheld from the public for several months because Roosevelt and his advisors were afraid that the Japanese in retaliation would prevent the *Gripsholm*, then en route, from delivering its materials to the POWs.[13] They were also fearful of Japanese reprisals against the POWs, and Secretary of State Cordell Hull announced that "America would hold Japan accountable for crimes committed against Japanese prisoners."[14]

Although my mother knew by then that my father had not been on the Death March, the further stories of atrocities could not have been reassuring. Meanwhile, thinking that he still had not heard from her, she redoubled her efforts to reach him, writing to the provost marshal general on March 20, 1944, asking the whereabouts of Camp #8. On the 28th he wrote back that he did not know.

On May 19, 1944, the Red Cross wrote to my mother requesting clarification of wording on a cable that she was trying to send (they wanted her "to state the relationship of 'Josie' to the prisoner of war") with some indication of bureaucratic confusion about which camp he was in. The cable was dispatched on June 5 (according to a Red Cross letter of July 12) and apparently received by my father in Camp #8 on August 5, 1944.[15] This was the last time that he heard from her until his repatriation in September 1945, nearly eighteen months later (the August letters had been written before the cable).

My mother received only one prison card from my father in the entire year of 1944. It arrived on August 18, stating, "Hope you are all well and not worrying too much about me. Josie must be a fine little girl by now." This card, however, had been written before he received her parcel (and thus sometime in 1943 or early 1944), and through the rest of 1944 she continued to believe that he had not heard from her at all since being captured. Significantly, in the section in my baby-book for "The Fourth Christmas," December 25, 1944, my mother entered only the year, "1944," leaving the rest of the space blank. Similarly, the section for my fourth birthday, March 10, 1945, was also left blank. This period (until summer 1945) was clearly the most difficult one of the war for her. Although, as noted, she received a final prison card on January 15, 1945—and another on January 22, 1945, in which he stated, "Just waiting for the day when I can be home with you, Josie, and all"—both had been mailed before he left the Philippines on the prison ship *Harō Maru*, October 1, 1944. By February 1945 she knew he had been on one of the prison ships, and she knew that some of them had been sunk.

The news of the sinking of the *Arisan Maru*, the "October ship," with its loss of eighteen hundred men, was announced to the American public in a United Press story dated February 16, 1945, in which one of eight survivors, Sgt. Avery Wilbur, described the October 24 sinking and his dramatic escape, which included several days in a small boat in the South China Sea and a lengthy overland journey through China.[16] My mother and uncle Joe immediately telephoned Avery in Appleton,

Wisconsin, trying to ascertain whether my father had
been on the torpedoed ship. Avery told them that he knew
my father, had been with him at Camp #8 and in Bilibid,
but that he had not seen or heard of him on the *Arisan
Maru.*

Soon after the liberation of the prisoner-of-war camps
in the Philippines (Bilibid was liberated on February 4,
1945), my mother wrote to various freed POW officers
whom she and my father had known before the war, asking for news of her husband, in particular whether he
had survived the prison ship voyage north. The first word
she received from a liberated POW came on March 9, on
a day my mother had been working at the Empire State
Building for the Red Cross. In her diary she notes: "Betty
Chandler got news from Franz Weissblatt that Bill
reached Japan safely. [Weissblatt] knew Bill. B. was on
'Port Area detail'—Got D.S.C. Left Philippines on
October convoy, definitely arrived. . . . They were
given warm Jap uniforms." A few days later she received
a letter from Weissblatt dated March 13, 1945, which,
though reassuring, contained, as it turned out, much
misinformation.

> United Press Associations
> News Building
> New York City
> March 13, 1945
> Dear Mrs. Donovan:
> I was glad to hear from you as I knew Bill quite well.
> I last saw him in October last year when he was
> brought in from detail. He was looking very well but
> possibly five pounds under his usual weight. This was
> not alarming considering conditions that we were liv-
> ing under. I am sure that his ship arrived in Japan
> safely. As a matter of fact—I spent most of yesterday
> with G2 [Intelligence] in Washington trying to coor-

dinate facts that I have with those in possession of
MIS [military intelligence sources, probably]. I be-
lieve that they are more or less assured that both the
October and December ships arrived in Japan safely.

They are very much interested, of course, as approximately 1,300 officers were on these two ships.

Bill was on detail most of the time that we were
in the Philippines. It was a small detail and life was
not very hard. It was made up of mechanics and the
Japs did not mistreat them too badly. Bill used to come
into Bilibid often with men who were ill (and he
would always give us some news—I mean authentic
news. However, I would not talk too much about that
angle as he is still in Jap hands and passing information among prisoners was frowned upon by our hosts.)

I can tell you that Bill's record on Bataan was excellent. I believe that he won the DSC. I am not quite
sure on that point but you probably have information on that. While in prison Bill continued his good
work as a Medical Officer and I know that his detail
was very much satisfied with Bill as not only a M.O.
[medical officer] but as a C.O. [commanding officer]
also.

His morale was always high and all in all I believe
that I can honestly say he acted as an officer and a
gentleman during the entire time commencing with
Pearl Harbor. As I said before, I am firmly convinced
that the October ship arrived in Japan okay. . . .

I believe that the port area was Camp No. 8 although I thought that Bill did some duty out in the
North area of the city also. In any case the details
only consisted of 50 men each and that made it nice
for the officers and men as not too many Japs were
around to make life miserable for them. . . .

Please come and see me when I get the leg fixed.
I will always be glad to see the families of the men
that went through that long ordeal in the Philippines.
I am only sorry that the 15,000 men still in the hands
of the Japs were not liberated when we were. I do

wish there was something that I could do about it. It seems so futile to just be able to tell wives, mothers and families "how sorry I feel for them." I realize that is not much comfort. The best that I can say to you now is to keep up your courage just as I am sure Bill and the rest of our men are doing.

My very best wishes to you
Franz Weissblatt

My mother also heard from Steve Sitter (March 15); Col. J. M. Weiss, who had talked to liberated prisoners Colonels Duckworth and Craig (March 16); Col. James W. Duckworth (April 12); Lester Fox (April 25); Col. Frank Adamo (May 27); and Col. Joseph S. Craig (July 9). All of these officers reported that they had known my father in prison camp, that he had been at Camp #8 in the port area, and that he had sailed on October 1, but none knew whether that ship had arrived safely. A letter from Gladys Peters, dated April 9, records her feelings upon the repatriation of her husband, Joe, and attempts to encourage my mother.

Dearest Dode,
Thanks for your nice letter. How we wish Bill could have come thru too. We are home now. It seems too good to be true. . . . Joe's condition is fairly good. He had dysentery 2 years and malaria as he was awfully thin. But is gaining now. He seems so thankful for everything.
He said Bill came to Bilibid Sept. 1944. His condition was good. He had had quite a bit of mail from you. He shipped out Oct. 1st.
Don't give up hope, Dode. Miracles can happen. We will continue to pray for Bill and for you to keep up courage.

Love
Glad & Joe

Meanwhile, momentous events were happening. Excerpts from my mother's and grandmother's 1945 diaries follow:

My mother:

April 12 President Roosevelt died.

April 14 Went to church, 4 P.M. Memorial service for Mr. Roosevelt.

May 8 V.E. Day—packed release kits for P.Ws in Europe

June 19 Eisenhower Day. Saw parade at 681 5th Ave. [my uncle André's office] & at Washington Square.

June 21 Sent Cable to Bill via Red Cross: "All well. Living for your return. Keep well. Love always, Dode"

My grandmother:

April 12 Shopped all morning. Got home to hear the shocking news of President Roosevelt's passing.

April 13 All very sad today as the details of Mr. Roosevelt's passing come in on the radio.

April 14 Dode, Josie, and I went to the service at Church of the Ascension at 3:30 P.M.

May 7 Peace is proclaimed in Europe. Germany has collapsed. Thank God.

May 8 Great rejoicing. Josie & I went to church & prayed for the speedy collapse of Japan so her Daddie could come home. Listened to all the Radio reports.

June 19 With all the family saw General Eisenhower [in a parade on Fifth Avenue] at our office & after at Washington Square Arch.

On July 1–2, my mother and I went by train to Madison, where we remained until November. The news that my mother had been anxiously waiting for—confirmation that my father had survived the prison ship journey from the Philippines—arrived on July 27, 1945, in a form letter dated the 25th from the provost marshal general's office, stating that the "above-named" had been transferred "to the camp indicated," Taihoku War Prisoners Camp, Taiwan (actually, he was at Shirakawa on Taiwan). The letter was sent to New York; my uncle André phoned my mother in Madison with the news. She recorded the event in her diary:

> July 27 André called: BILL SAFE ON FORMOSA.

My grandmother (in New York) noted:

> July 28 News from W.D. Bill is on Formosa. Thank God. We are all very happy. Just so happy!!!
> July 30 Letter from Dode. Is she happy!

The end of the war is recorded in my mother's diary as follows:

> Aug 6 ATOMIC BOMB
> Aug 8 Russia declares war on Japan
> Aug 10 Japs surrender offer via Stockholm & Berne to US, Eng, China, Russia
> Aug 12 False surrender
> Aug 14 *Japan surrenders*. God bless my Bill & bring him home soon safe & sound.

My grandmother noted:

> Aug 13 Heard news of false surrender. Phoned Dode.
> Aug 14 Real Armistice Day . . . Town [New York City] is in an uproar.

The long wait was not over, however. My mother had yet to hear directly from my father (she had not heard from him since the cards written nearly a year before, which she had received in January). On August 31 a form telegram from the War Department informed her that WHILE NO INFORMATION HAS YET BEEN RECEIVED AS TO THE RETURN TO MILITARY CONTROL OF YOUR HUSBAND . . . YOU ARE INVITED TO SUBMIT A MESSAGE NOT TO EXCEED TWENTY-

FIVE WORDS FOR ATTEMPTED DELIVERY TO HIM AT SUCH TIME AS HE RETURNS TO MILITARY CONTROL PERIOD . . . My mother immediately sent the cable, but it was returned undelivered. She had sent a "liberation letter" on August 17, but it, too, was lost.

At 8:30 A.M. on September 13 the long-awaited cable from my father (then in Manila) finally arrived in Madison:

> HOME SOON WAIT ME NEW YORK OR MADISON SEND WORD YOURS FAMILYS HEALTH COMPLETED MEDICAL EXAMINATION HEALTH PERFECT ALL MY LOVE WILLIAM DONAVAN [*sic*]

My mother described the event in her first letter to him after his liberation, but it was returned undelivered:

> September 13, 1945
> My darling,
> . . . Thank God you are safe, thank God you are well, thank God you are coming home!
> Janet brought up your telegram when I was still in bed. Grandma[,] Elly[,] & the kids all congregated, Joe jumped out of the tub & Josie said, "Let's go to Sweet's [the corner grocery] & get lots of food for Papa." We all laughed & cried . . .
>
> Love always & forever—
> your wife Dode

No return cables were getting through to my father, although my mother and other family members repeatedly sent cables and letters to him in Manila. In turn, he kept wiring them (on September 15, 17, and 18) for news. Finally, he cabled his brother Tony, a doctor in the U.S. Public Health Service stationed in Lima, Peru, who wired his brother Joe, in Madison, urging that they wire my father, which, of course, they were trying to do. My mother then contacted various government officials, including Leo Crowley, a family friend and an official in the Roosevelt administration, and Senator La Follette, in an attempt to access governmental communication channels, but all to no avail. Fortunately, though, just before he left Manila on September 18, my father received a short letter, dated August 5, sent to Taihoku, Taiwan, from my mother. And, on September 25 aboard the USS *Hugh Rodman* bound for the United States, he received a telegram from my mother reassuring him that everyone was fine and eagerly awaiting his arrival.

Meanwhile, my mother received ten letters, a selection from which follows. My father had written almost daily from the time of his arrival in Manila on September 6 until their reunion in Chicago.

> Manila, P.I.
> 7 Sept 45
> write: 312th Gen Hosp
> c/o Det of Patients
> APO 75 c/o PM
> San Francisco, Cal.
> My own darling wife:
> At last I'm free and back in Manila, arriving last night by plane from Formosa. It's impossible to describe the marvelous feeling of being free and knowing that very soon I will be with you and Josie again. . . . It is over a year since I've had any word from you but I trust and pray that you, Josie, and our families are well, and that Ma is in good health.
>   My health is remarkably good. I had a complete physical examination this morning and aside from loss of weight everything was normal. I weighed 136 lbs so a few weeks of good food will bring me up to the 150 lbs I usually weigh. In other words when I arrive home I think you'll find me very little changed from the husband you last saw on that sad day of May 14, 1941. . . . My thoughts and love have been constantly with you all through this period. . . . And planning

for the grand day of our reunion and of our life together has been always foremost in my thoughts and
heart. And that day of reunion is now very close. All
evacuees are being sent to hospitals as they arrive, for
a physical checkup, vaccinations, clothing issues, etc.,
which accounts for my being in this hospital. I have
been doing professional work in POW hospitals all
through this period until yesterday when doctors arrived and took over the work. I left Taihoku, Formosa
last evening 4:15 and arrived here at 8:45 P.M. It is
amazing, the care and effort that is being devoted to
the POW's as they are freed. Absolutely everything
that could possibly be done is being done.

I'm writing Ma by this mail. I am just waiting to
be with all of you. Can't wait to see and become acquainted with our little daughter, Josie. I send my
love to all our families, Ma, Mother, Joe, Tony, Marie,
Elly, the kids, and all. And all my love to you . . .

Bill

Liberated Personnel Section
APO 501 c/o Postmaster
San Francisco, Cal
14 Sept 45
Manila, P.I.
My own beloved wife,
I've sent several cables and letters so you should know
by now that I am alive and well. So far I've received
no word from you or the folks at home and I am anxiously waiting for word that you, Josie, Ma, Mother
and all the family are well. Send a cablegram and air
mail letter to the above address as soon as possible. I
simply can't wait to hear from you to know that you
and Josie are all right. My last word from you was
April 44 a radiogram which arrived on my birthday.[17]
I've been thinking of you constantly . . . all this long
period of our separation. And it's been your love and
my love for you that has sustained me. I know that in
many ways it has been worse for you at home, with

the terrible worry and uncertainty always present, than
it has been for me. I have tried not to worry unduly
about you during the last 4 years. But now that I am
free I am just aching to get word that you and Josie
are all right. The moments when that word is received
will be the happiest of my life. I've been through
some pretty tight places in the past few years and
thank God have come through unscathed and in excellent shape. I only pray to God that you are well
and that soon we will be able to take up our good life
together. . . .

During this time, my mother wrote twelve letters and
sent three cables. Other family members also sent seven
letters, but only two or three of the letters and one cable
reached him before his return to Madison. In her letters
my mother reflects on her experiences on the home front,
her gratitude at his good condition, and her annoyance
at the red tape that has prevented him from receiving his
family's letters and cables.

> September 15, 1945
> My own darling Bill,
> . . . As for me I guess I am the same tho' 5 years older,
> of course. . . . It has been a *long* time without you but
> when I think of what it must have been for you, how
> can I complain? I had Josie & family & comfort. We
> never missed a thing all through the war & don't let
> anyone tell you we did. We had all the food & cloth-
> ing we needed . . . how fortunate I am that you are
> coming home. So many are not!!
>
> Your Dode
>
> Sunday, September 16, 1945
> My own darling Bill
> . . . There is so much about your life the last years I
> don't know it will be like being newlyweds again. . . .
> Josie said to me yesterday: "I'm lucky my Papa didn't

get wounded in the war; all the other kids' papas
did.". . .

Your own Dode

The *Rodman* arrived in San Francisco on October 3,
whereupon my father called my mother in Madison. In a
follow-up letter dated 2:30 P.M., October 3, he wrote,
"Just finished talking to you a few minutes ago . . . and
how wonderful it was to hear your voice. I can't tell you
how happy I am. . . . Josie . . . said she remembered me.
It will be so marvelous to be together again." My mother
also wrote immediately after the call: "Oh Bill, I still can't
believe that I have spoken to you, that the nightmare
really is over." In another letter the next day my mother
notes, "Isn't it silly that I should be so terribly impatient
& anxious to get to you? You'd think I'd be used to
waiting."

On October 5, in the last letter she wrote before their
reunion, October 9, my mother recounted the fates of
some of their friends.

> Thelma Black is anxious to see you when you have
> had a chance to relax. I don't know if you heard about
> Fred. He is carried as having gone down on the prison
> ship going to Japan from the P. I. October 24 last.
> Thelma didn't know about it until this July. Those
> ships were among the most horrible events of all
> these war years. . . . Kathryn Hagen wrote Ken had
> been in a Nagasaki Mine [when the atomic bomb was
> dropped]. . . . Maxie Noble is unaccounted for. He
> was with the guerillas[,] was finally captured[,] was
> in Bilibid till early 1944 when he was removed and
> Evelyn doesn't know what happened then. Up until a
> few days ago she had had no news. [Max Noble was
> executed in Bilibid.] Eddie Wright was not captured
> but hid on Bataan until last February.

On the same day, October 5, while still in San Francisco, my father reflected in a letter to my mother (his last to her before their reunion) on his medical experiences in prison camp and on his own determination to survive. Noting that released prisoners were required to undergo an intense physical exam, he wrote:

> It's a good thing as many of them are pretty well run down. I've been on duty professionally taking care of prisoners all through the prison period. All the doctors, practically, were in the same category and we were able to keep busy, keep our minds occupied, and at the same time avoid the hard work the men had to do. In my last camp we had a nice library and I read medical and other books I would never have had time to do. I was able to read complete texts in Medicine, Surgery, Pathology, and Physiology. So that, coupled with the fact that I always had 40 to 50 patients to look after, makes me feel that I'm pretty much up professionally. There have been new drugs, etc. but if a person knows the fundamentals of medicine, therapeutics is very easy to learn.
>
> Another reason why I am in good shape is that I was able to avoid diseases to a large extent by being careful of water, etc. while many of the men didn't care or didn't realize the dangers. And if I did start to come down with something I took care of it immediately and recovered in a hurry. Because with you and Josie waiting for me I just had to come back. I just had to.

Notes

1. Unless otherwise indicated, all documentation in this chapter are to materials in the personal possession of the authors.

2. Juanita Redmond, *I Served on Bataan* (Philadelphia: Lippincott, 1943). Redmond's narrative appears to have been a primary source for the movie *So Proudly We Hail* (1943), which was made about the nurses on Bataan and Corregidor and starred

Claudette Colbert, Paulette Goddard, and Veronica Lake. Colonel Thomas W. Doyle, my father's commanding officer on Bataan, served as technical adviser for the film, which is noted for its authenticity, after his escape from Corregidor (see Chapter 2).

3. Daws, *Prisoners of the Japanese*, 128–29.

4. Kerr, *Surrender and Survival*, 189.

5. Ibid., 190. See also Earl Archibald Fitzgerald, *Voices in the Night* (Bellingham, WA: Pioneer Printing, 1948).

6. See especially Roland, "Allied POWs."

7. *New York Times*, February 13, 1944, 16.

8. Daws, *Prisoners of the Japanese*, 128.

9. Kerr, *Surrender and Survival*, 12.

10. Hayes, *Bilibid Diary*, 132.

11. *New York Times*, January 28, 1944, 1.

12. Spector, *Eagle against the Sun*, 398.

13. *New York Times*, February 2, 1944, 5.

14. Knox, *Death March*, 269n.

15. The extant radiogram appears to have been sent on his birthday, April 24, 1944, but was received on August 5, 1944. On the envelope of another letter my father wrote: "Radiogram received 8-5-44. Daughter Josie, Ma everyone well sending birthday love awaiting return wife Dode Donovan." My father continued to receive mail at Camp #8 until late August 1944, but this correspondence had been written prior to April 1944; thus, the April radiogram was the latest word he had received from the family.

16. *New York World-Telegram*, February 16, 1945. In the *New York Times* account, February 16, 1945, Avery said that the ship left Manila on October 11 and was torpedoed thirteen days later: "We were jammed into two holds, with 1,200 in the one I was placed. The ship was cut in two by the explosion. I ran up and walked right off the deck into the water. I had a life jacket on and I managed to stay afloat until I got on a lifeboat on which was one man. Three others later got on it with us and we floated for three days before we reached shore. . . . When the torpedo struck, guards ignored us and hundreds of us Americans got into the water but the Japs wouldn't let us in their lifeboats. They beat us off with clubs." See also Manny Lawson, *Some Survived* (Chapel Hill, NC: Algonquin, 1984), 124–25, for another account of this dramatic story.

17. See note 15.

Appendix

Deposition for the War Crimes Office, Judge Advocate General's Department, U.S. War Department, made by Major William Nelson Donovan on February 10, 1947, Columbia, South Carolina.

" On 1 October 1944 at the Port of Embarkation at Manila, while standing in line to board [the *Harō Maru*] I observed Lieutenant Nogi, Chief Japanese Medical Officer in charge of medical aspects in the Philippine Islands and a two (2) star general, Japanese army, name unknown . . . [who was] I believe . . . in charge of all Prisoners of War Camps in the Philippines from July 1944 until October 1944. They were inspecting this ship and presumably gave it their O.K. Shortly after completing their inspection we boarded the ship. The Prisoners of War were put in two (2) holds, the larger measuring twenty by twenty-five (20 by 25) yards and about twenty (20) yards in depth. The floor of this hold was covered with coal and a small supply of newspaper and plain paper was furnished, presumably toilet paper ration for the trip. The detail consisted of approximately one thousand (1,000) Prisoners of War. Six hundred (600) were put in the forward (large) hold and the remainder in rear hold approximately one-half size of forward hold.

I was in the [forward] hold for the first night and in the [rear] hold for the remainder of the trip. The conditions in both holds were similar as far as space was concerned; only two-thirds of the group could be seated at a time and the remainder had to stand. This condition existed throughout the trip. [As] soon as the Prisoners of War were all aboard, the hatch openings were covered by large planks, six (6) by eight (8) inch planks, spaced two to three inches apart, thus preventing any circulation of air, [which] kept the hold at a point of suffocation. The method of exit consisted of a small iron ladder which on climbing you had to climb straight up and backwards. The latrine privileges were allowed to two (2) men at a time during the day and one (1) man at a time during the night to use the deck latrine. The removal of human waste was cared for by lowering a bucket, which was passed around and pulled back up and dumped over board. The rope on this bucket soon became rotten, and it was common to have the rope break and spill the contents over the entire group of Prisoners of War.

The method of distributing water, theoretically one (1) canteen of water per day for each man, [was as follows:] the canteens set around on the floor of the hold amidst human waste and were gathered up by a detail of two (2) or three (3) men and carried up to the deck. [They] were refilled without exteriors being washed by being submerged into large buckets. The contents were polluted and added greatly to the spread of diarrhea and dysentery. Often this operation was halted by the Japanese before all of the canteens were filled, while plenty of water remained in the buckets for this purpose. The method of distributing food was by lowering a bucket and the distribution was made by the Prisoners of War. At no time were any provisions made for the Prisoners of War to wash their mess gears. The food was lowered by rope and bucket twice a day in theory, and often the rope would break and cause hot rice to fall on the Prisoners causing severe burns that became infected because of the lack of medical supplies. Upon leaving Manila the Japanese took ten (10) percent of the Red Cross medical supplies and allowed us only ten (10) percent of the original ten (10) percent taken aboard by the Japanese. This meager supply lasted about twelve (12) or fifteen (15) days. Then we were without medical supplies which were desperately needed. . . .

Several of us requested the Japanese Lieutenant in charge to have the boards over the hatches removed, to give us salt, more water, and more medical supplies, which were on board and available. We also asked him to allow sick men on deck and a percent of the men to sleep on deck. This was refused and about the second or third time we requested the same the Japanese Lieutenant brought forth what he told us to be a Japanese order and stated that he had been ordered to comply with this written order, because he had been in charge of bringing prisoners of war from the vicinity of Mindanao to Manila and had been lenient with the Prisoners of War and several of them escaped by diving overboard. He had been censured for this and as [a] result he was given specific orders from higher authority on the handling of this ship.

There occurred thirty-four (34) deaths among the Prisoners of War the first ten days and after this condition had been explained to the Japanese Lieutenant in charge he allowed a few men on deck but it was too late and the harm had been done. The Japanese Lieutenant would not allow me on deck with my patients. The only patients allowed on deck were those who had passed out in the hold and had to be hauled to the deck by rope. This Japanese Officer seemed to have it in for medical officers in particular and would not allow supervision of the sick Prisoners of War on deck. This attitude changed after several deaths occurred amongst the Prisoners of War. The first twenty deaths were buried without formality; they were placed in a blanket and thrown overboard. We tried to get a Chaplain but were refused this request. Those who died near Hong Kong or in Hong Kong were taken ashore, dressed, and buried. The Japanese Lieutenant in charge was responsible for the methods of burial. The planks covering the hatches were never removed but we did receive a little salt and more water later in the trip. During the early part of the trip I tried to see the Japanese Lieutenant in charge but was refused. The way I finally contacted him was every time a death occurred I had to go up and fill out a death certificate and it was during this time that I got to see him. I asked if I could hold sick call on deck and that a percent of the Prisoners be allowed on deck. This was refused at first but later in the trip this request was allowed.

Beatings occurred every day, which were chiefly slapping done by Japanese guards. . . . [One] perpetrator would strike men as they entered and left the latrine; this was done for no apparent reason. If the men were making noise in the hold, [this] guard [would close] the top of the hatch and stop everyone from going to the latrine. A Taiwanese three (3) star private, who was in charge of the front hold . . . frequently struck Prisoners of War with his fists. This did not occur often, [but] he had a terrific temper. On one occasion this guard struck Lieutenant Thwaites eight (8) or ten (10) times about the face. . . .

When we reached a port in Southern Formosa and while waiting to disembark, two (2) Japanese medical corpsmen made stool examinations of the Prisoners of War. Men were lined up on the deck of the ship and a dry glass rod was rammed up their rectums for stool culturing. The Dutch and English Prisoners of War who had been on board since February were in the worst shape and had [a] hard time getting out of the hold to the deck. They and American Prisoners of War were shoved along and beaten by Japanese guards because they could not move fast enough. If they fell down they were kicked and beaten. This went on one entire day on or about the 30th or 31st of October 1944. . . .

At the harbor of [Takao] in southern Formosa four (4) Prisoners of War (Americans) were brought aboard the [ship] from a Japanese destroyer. They were left on deck, exposed to cold rain, periodically beaten. One of these men died, his name was Hughes; the death occurred during the night of 8th and 9th November 1944, while en route to Shiragawa on a train. In my opinion Hughes's death occurred as result of this mistreatment. After the first twenty-four hours these men had been aboard, the Japanese put out an order that anyone caught communicating with or signalling these men would be shot. . . .

When we disembarked at [Takao] they wanted a list of the most seriously ill and we told them that no one was able to march over a block or two. They insisted on this list, which we put in with a large number of names, [but the] list was cut in size by the Japanese. The next morning the order to disembark was given. They ran everyone over the side of the ship into small boats regardless of illness or ailments. After landing we had to march to a quarantine area, then back to the dock and [be] placed in small boats, an overall distance of approximately one (1) mile. The boats we were placed in were twenty (20) to twenty-four (24) feet in length. The Japanese guard placed forty (40) Prisoners of War in the boat and told them in Japanese to move forward and kneel down. The Prisoners of War did not understand this order and the guard picked up a boat hook and beat them over the heads until they knelt down and then continued beating them on the back. The name and description of this guard is unknown to me as I was too busy ducking the blows. . . ."[1]

Major Donovan's deposition does not appear to have actually been used in the Tokyo War Crimes Trials, as the "hell ship" testimony was presented in mid-December 1946,[2] and the deposition was submitted in February 1947. The treatment of the prisoners on the ships was considered a "Crime against Humanity" under the terms of the indictment.

Notes

1. Deposition by Major William Nelson Donovan, February 10, 1947, Item #67-138, Record Group 153, National Archives, College Park, MD.

2. Brackman, *The Other Nuremberg*, 260. Also, the Tokyo trial was of A-class criminals, whereas the individuals implicated in Major Donovan's testimony were probably considered B- or C-class. The latter were tried in Yokohama, Japan, and elsewhere.